DYNAMIC PREACHING

DYNAMIC PREACHING

Chevis F. Horne

BROADMAN PRESS
Nashville, Tennessee

Dewey Decimal Classification: 251
Subject heading: PREACHING
Library of Congress Catalog Card No.: 82-70871
Printed in the United States of America

Dedication

To my late parents, the Reverend Claude Broadus and Ressie
Simmons Horne, my brother Melton, my sister Mildred, and
my Aunt Nell, whose love I have never doubted and in whose
full acceptance I have always felt secure

FOREWORD

In *Dynamic Preaching,* Dr. Chevis Horne has put all who would preach the gospel, and all who would hear it clearly, in his debt. It is hardly possible to read a single page of this book without beginning to realize that here we have a treasure, rich and ennobling, which will adorn and benefit the company of preachers for a long time to come.

Dr. Horne writes from within his long experience of preaching and hearing preaching. Here is no novice, but a workman whose skills and art have been honed and perfected through many years of distinguished pulpit work. Doubtless, the rich ore Dr. Horne has mined and which he shares so generously here will save many a fledgling preacher much fruitless search for an effective way to make available to people "the unsearchable riches of Christ."

The central strength, one thinks, of this book is its loyalty to the endless, living insights resident in all of the Bible. This strength is married to inspired disclosure of how these insights address themselves so directly to our lives that "surprise," "luster," and "appeal" become powerful weapons in the preacher's arsenal. These transcripts from the pulpit experience of a master workman will instruct, inspire, and delight preachers in a way hard to exaggerate.

Preaching is almost always done in troublous times, since "man that is born of a woman is of few days, and full of trouble." Remembering this, anyone who reads this book will not soon forget the tested and proven methods it suggests in regard to preaching to people in their most vulnerable moments. Likewise, there will be indelible impression of the realism and honesty which it contains while touched at the same time by a tenderness of manner and a sweetness of spirit born of the shepherd's heart.

GARDNER TAYLOR

PREFACE

Paul said the gospel "is the power of God unto salvation" (Rom. 1:16). The gospel is the dynamite *(dunamis)* of God. Preaching is proclaiming the good news of the gospel. When preaching is weak and ineffective you would like to ask the preacher: "Do you know what you hold in your hands? You hold dynamite. Why don't you explode it? Detonate it! Set it off!"

Preaching should be dynamic and the pulpit should be a place of power. But alas, this is not always so. The sermon may have structure but not vitality. It may be like a "dud" that does not explode. Preaching can be like those carcasses Ezekiel saw on the desert sands. They had perfect form but they did not live.

This book is concerned with making preaching effective. It seeks to answer the vital question: What makes preaching dynamic?

I have suggested the following guidelines for making preaching dynamic.

First, preach the Word of God. We declare this significant affirmation: God has spoken. He has broken the terrible silence about life's ultimate meaning. His word, like light, has pierced the darkness and mystery that surround us. Indeed, he has spoken the decisive word without which we cannot live. The word we preach comes from beyond us. It has been revealed to us; it has been given to us.

Second, put the Word of God into human speech. This we can do since God has spoken in events of history, through persons, and through the Person, Jesus Christ. God has spoken his final word in clearest accent through Jesus of Nazareth. Use the kind of language the Bible does—vivid, concrete, picturesque. Preaching should make use of metaphors, similes, imagery, and analogies. A preacher should be an artist painting pictures with words. Ideas should have visual power.

Third, the gospel must be experienced by the preacher. It should be good news to him. The truth of the gospel should pass through his or her life the way sunlight does through a stained glass window. The window could never be the source of the light. The source is the heavens, but as the sunlight takes on itself the luster of the stained glass, just so the gospel should be clothed with the warmth and humanity of the preacher.

Fourth, preaching has a human target, and therefore to be relevant the gospel must be addressed to people. It should be addressed to the whole person—mind, heart, and will. The gospel should speak to those deep, permanent levels of life where people always stand, but it must also be directed to them where they stand shakily amid the shifting scenes of the present moment. The gospel should speak to their personal, social, and corporate lives.

Fifth, preaching should make use of the imagination. Few capacities have the power to touch biblical truth to life the way the imagination can. You recreate the historical situation and then enter it imaginatively. You were there when it happened. You stand with people through those great moments. You see with them and you feel with them. You laugh with them and you weep with them. You hope with them and you despair with them. The ancient word becomes a living word which you transpose into today's life. However, there is one note of caution: Don't use your imagination irresponsibly. Keep it tied to reality.

Sixth, let preaching be empowered by the Holy Spirit. Just as only the Spirit of God could breathe life into those lifeless bodies which Ezekiel saw, so only the Holy Spirit can fill our homiletical forms—sterile and lifeless as they frequently are—with vitality and power. Just as the Holy Spirit made preaching so powerful in the early church, he can turn the modern pulpit, which is often so weak, into a place of power.

If this book can contribute toward making preaching more dynamic and the pulpit more powerful, I shall be happy beyond measure.

CHEVIS F. HORNE

CONTENTS

1
Addressing the Whole Person

We have a whole gospel for the whole person. The gospel is to be addressed to the mind, heart, and will. If anyone of these is overemphasized or neglected, preaching becomes distorted. If the mind alone is addressed, preaching will be cold; if only the heart, preaching will be little more than emotional froth; if only the will, preaching will lay a burden on people too heavy to be borne. People need to think the gospel, feel the gospel, and do the gospel.

THE MIND

The human mind is a wonderful instrument. It can be brilliant, searching, probing, analytical, perceptive, and creative. We often stand amazed before mankind's mental powers.

The psalmist saw man dwarfed against his universe. He seemed so small and insignificant. Yet, there was a grandeur about him that was not enjoyed by anything else in God's creation. "Thou has made him a little less than God," the psalmist exclaimed; "and dost crown him with glory and honor. Thou hast given him dominion over the work of thy hands, thou hast put all things under his feet" (Ps. 8:5-6). Why was God able to give man and woman dominion over the works of his hands? Because they are rational creatures.

An astronomer studying the heavens cried out: "I am reading God's thoughts after him!" It was a legitimate exclamation. The human mind is wonderful. If we fail to address it, we do not speak to one of the unique dimensions of human life. It is little wonder that Jesus affirmed we are to love God with our *minds*.

There are at least four reasons why we should address the mind in our preaching.

First, the mind makes theological reflection possible. Living theology never begins with abstract truth. It begins with meeting, encounter, experience. Theology is experience before it is doctrine and dogma. Having had experience, we ask two questions: What is the meaning of this, and how can I communicate it intelligibly? In answering those questions, theology occurs.

Take, for example, the doctrine of the Trinity. Before it was doctrine, it was experience. That is the way we have known God. We have encountered him as Trinity. We have known him as Father and Creator who is above us. We have known him as Jesus the Son who is back of us in our history. We have known him as Holy Spirit who is in our world, present with us. Therefore, we have experienced God as above us, back of us, and with us. It was only as the mind reflected critically on our experiences of God that we articulated the doctrine of the Trinity. We should remember that the Trinity in the New Testament lies somewhere between experience and a carefully formed doctrine. We have something more than experience but something less than rigid dogma.

It is easy to have a bias against theology. It may seem to be too cloistered, too abstract, and too out of touch with life. I had that kind of prejudice against theology when I entered the seminary. Christian ethics appealed to me but not Christian theology. I couldn't wait for critical reflection. I was a practical man and I was in a hurry. I wanted to get on with changing the world. But I found out better—I had to learn the wisdom that Paul knew so well. He knew that ethics should not be divorced from theology, that it is perilous to separate action from faith. In his letters he dealt with theology and ethics, but theology came first. He wrote about how they were to believe and then in the light of that how they were to live. Christian theology is the soil that grows and nurtures Christian ethics. Therefore, when Christian ethics are uprooted from their soil, they become like cut flowers. They wither and die.

We should remember that neither the pulpit nor the pew can escape the theological task, since theology is an understanding of God and his relationship with us and our world. We are all theologians, whether good ones or poor ones. It is certain that all of us will be poor ones if we fail to address the mind in our preaching.

Second, the mind helps make the gospel intelligible and communicable. It is true that the mind comes quickly upon frontiers beyond which it cannot pass. Beyond those frontiers lie mystery and the unknown. If truth comes from there, it has to be revealed, disclosed. Christianity is basically a religion of revelation, and its truth is disclosed to us by God. Our truth as Christians comes from beyond those frontiers of mystery. Our truth essentially is not rational, abstract, or propositional. We don't discover it in our rational powers. But this does not mean that Christian truth is irrational, unreasonable, and unspeakable. It can be expressed in rational, intelligible, and human terms. But how?

The voice that speaks from mystery can use our speech. The truth is revealed in human and historical events. The supreme revelation has occurred in a person who stepped across those frontiers of mystery into the light of our common day. He is Jesus Christ, and he has walked on our dusty roads and used our human speech. But that does not relieve us of our intellectual task. We need to make our gospel as intelligible as we can and communicate it as clearly as possible. That takes work.

Our gospel is not made for lazy minds. We will have to use our minds, and we will have to appeal to the minds of our hearers. It is unfortunate when the sermon is not intellectually stimulating. It is tragic when the congregation leaves saying to themselves: "The sermon didn't make sense." We need to heed the admonition offered to Timothy: "Do your best to present yourself to God as one approved, a workman who has no need to be ashamed, rightly handling the word of truth" (2 Tim. 2:15).

Third, the mind helps prevent religion from being vulnerable to superstition and fanaticism. Religion can be most vulnerable to superstition. Often superstition, like a heavy mist, can lie across the landscape of religion. It is easy to get faith and magic confused.

I was a chaplain during World War II, and I often saw soldiers treat their Bibles as if they had some magical power. Some of them would go into combat wearing their New Testaments over their hearts as if they were charms. How sad it often was to see them brought to a collection point on the highway —with their New Testaments still on their bodies.

We use "magic" as a power by which we try to manipulate God. Reason helps us to understand that authentic religion lies not in using God but in a relationship of trust with him. It is not so much using God as it is letting God use us.

Religion is also more vulnerable to fanaticism than most things I know. It can so easily go to extremes and excesses. A nationally-known magazine several years ago told a pathetic story about an eleven-year-old boy dying when he shouldn't have. He was a diabetic, and was taken off insulin after he and his parents went to a faith-healing service where it was believed he had been healed. The boy lapsed into a state of unconsciousness after two days, and the father would not let him be put back on insulin. Soon the boy died. His funeral was the starkest and most depressing scene possible. Only the undertaker and the gravedigger were there. The parents, remaining at home, believed their son would be resurrected. Finally, the devil was blamed for it all.

This is an extreme example, but even in sophisticated religion there are often ideas which, if carried to their logical conclusion, would end in fanaticism.

The intellect, dedicated to Christ, can stand like a strong dike against the floodwaters of religious fanaticism and irrationality.

Fourth, the intellect can help save us from the dangers of a blind, literalistic, and irresponsible interpretation of the Bible. We can naïvely insist: "The Bible says it, and that's it." When we do that, sooner or later we have the Bible contradicting itself or saying things that shock the moral sensibilities of good people. God can be made to say and do things that decent human beings would not do or say.

One of the great gifts of modern scholarship is the historical approach to the Bible. Some people fear it, but they should not. What a wonderful tool it is in the control of the mind.

I remember talking with a member of a sect who came to the field where I was working as a boy. He told me there was no future life, that death marks the end of existence for humans as it does for animals. Then he quoted Ecclesiastes 3:19: "For that which befalleth the sons of men befalleth beasts; even one thing befalleth them: as the one dieth, so dieth the other; yea, they have all one breath; so that a man hath no preeminence above a beast: for all is vanity" (KJV).

I was really confused. There it was in the Bible, and I believed the Bible in a very literal way. Yet, I believed in the resurrection of Jesus, and I remembered how often the New Testament spoke of eternal life. I seemed to face an impasse with no exit. I was severely troubled. There would have been no problem for me if I had known the historical approach to the Bible. Then I would have understood that Ecclesiastes is about a man on a pilgrimage from cynicism to faith, and along that way he made the statement about a man being like a beast.

TO THE HEART

A strong appeal must be made to the heart since it is the dynamic center of life. We are more heart than head. How often we use our minds to justify how our hearts feel about something.

Last summer I was at a nationally known conference center which invites the best preachers of the nation to be the conference pastor for a week at a time. The preacher for the week was well known. He was biblically grounded and he was in touch with his world. He was also a good homiletician, knowing how to construct a sermon, and he sought new and fresh forms for the gospel. He was a sensitive man and cared for people. Yet, he did not grip his hearers. I asked a very active layman, why? He pointed to his heart and said: "He doesn't reach me here."

The mind untouched by the heart can be cold. The sermon that is purely intellectual does not move a congregation. Such a sermon can be like a winter's night. It leaves the people emotionally chilled. It is one of the best ways to empty a sanctuary.

We should be careful that the mind and heart are not at variance with each other in our preaching. When they are, the heart wins, and the power of the mind is lost on the hearers. "When the intellectual and emotional modes are at variance with each other," observe Stevenson and Diehl, "people instinctively choose the emotional message and disregard the intellectual."[1]

Even as the heart keeps the mind from being cold, it is the heart that spurs the will to action. It is the heart that builds a fire beneath a sluggish will and gets it moving. Only feeling can move the will to strong action.

Randy Goodrum, a modern songwriter, says, "In writing a

song, I think of an emotion, not an idea." While the preacher begins with an idea, not an emotion, he can learn much from Goodrum about the importance and power of feeling.

When I was a boy growing up in Eastern North Carolina, the test of a good sermon was a simple one: Did it bring tears? If it didn't, leaving the eyes of the congregation dry, it wasn't much of a sermon. I reacted against that kind of emotionalism. When I finished the seminary, I wanted my sermons to be well-thought-out, rational, and logical, appealing to the intellect and not the feelings. I was very foolish. With the passing of the years, I learned: that simple criterion for preaching was not without its values. It, of course, has to be balanced with two other criteria: Does it stimulate the mind? and does it move the will? If the heart is not moved the mind remains cold and the will sluggish.

How do you stir the heart in preaching? Let me make four suggestions.

First, preach the gospel authentically. The gospel is not about abstract ideas. It is about a Person who "dwelt among us." He laughed and wept, knew joy and sadness, suffered and died. You cannot meet him and be unmoved by him as if he were an abstraction. You respond feelingly to Jesus.

The central truths of our faith as well, as the language in which they are expressed, have strong emotional overtones. God is love; not only is God love, love is what he does. "For God so loved the world that he gave his only Son, that whoever believes in him should not perish but have eternal life" (John 3:16). Even the call to the ethical life has feeling in it: "A new commandment I give to you, that you love one another even as I have loved you, that you also love one another. By this all men will know that you are my disciples, if you have love for one another" (John 13:34-35).

When the gospel is preached authentically, it speaks to us where we are emotionally sensitive. It touches the deepest springs of our hearts. It speaks to our loneliness and separation, our alienation and rebellion, our fears and anxiety. It speaks to our hopes, our deep longings, and our insatiable desire for God. It speaks to us where we are threatened, fleeing, seeking a place of refuge. It is the voice of a loving Father calling us home.

Second, share your heart with those to whom you preach. The truth borne on the strength of feeling will be most deeply heard and longest remembered. Share your anguish and your joy.

This doesn't mean that you are tearful in the pulpit. It doesn't mean that you are always holding an emotional wound before your congregation, saying "See how I am hurting." It means that you are to be human. To be human is to hurt and hope. This will shine through your preaching.

Ezekiel related a most unusual experience in his life. "So I spoke to the people in the morning, and at evening my wife died. And on the next morning I did as I was commanded" (Ezek. 24:18). I am sure that those who heard Ezekiel's sermon the morning after his wife died were never able to forget it. How could they forget the hurt in his eyes and the pain in his voice?

Rodney (Gipsy) Smith (1860-1947) was one of the most widely acclaimed preachers of his generation. (Gipsy is the correct spelling.) He was born in a gypsy tent in England, lost his mother when he was a child, and was without formal theological education. Yet, he claimed five continents for his parish. One of the secrets of his greatness in the pulpit was his ability to appeal to the heart. John Clifford wrote of him: "Exhaustless resources of pathos are his. There is a tear in his voice. He moves the heart of his audience to its utmost depths."[2]

George W. Truett was one of the greatest preachers I have ever heard. Two things I shall never forget about him. He had the most powerful platform presence I have ever known. When he entered the pulpit area a hush fell over his audience. And I can never forget his deep, full, resonant voice which had pathos in it. Truett and Smith were alike at this point: There was a tear in their voices.

Many great sermons have been preached, but only the rarest are kept, remembered, and treasured by the church. One of those rare sermons is A. J. Gossip's, "But When Life Tumbles In, What Then?" It was preached the Sunday after he had buried his wife. Those who heard that sermon could not forget the anguish and hope they felt in it. You can't read it without being moved by it. History will not forget it.

John Claypool lost a beautiful daughter with leukemia when she was ten. He and his wife stood by that lovely child for months and saw her die a slow death. I heard John preach one evening at Princeton Theological Seminary when he told about losing his daughter. His text was from Isaiah 40:31: "But they who wait for the Lord shall renew their strength,/they shall mount up with wings like eagles,/they shall run and not be weary,/they shall walk and not faint." He told of the anguish of those months and of the hope and faith that sustained him and his wife. Those of us who heard that sermon can never forget it. He moved our hearts.

Third, be concrete in your preaching. We are not ubiquitous—we are not everywhere. We are somewhere. We live our lives in concrete situations. Sermons that address the situations in which we live our lives are most moving.

That is how Jesus preached. For example, when he talked about lostness he did not do it in an abstract sort of manner. He didn't give an essay on it. He told about a lost sheep, a lost coin, and a lost son. Have you ever stopped to think about the strong emotional element in these stories?

The shepherds called together his friends and said: "Rejoice with me, for I have found my sheep which was lost" (Luke 15:6). The woman called in her neighbors and said to them: "Rejoice with me, for I have found the coin which I had lost"

(Luke 15:9). The father of the lost boy had a banquet quickly prepared. There to his right was the guest of honor, the profligate son who had returned home. The father said to his guests: "My son was dead, and is alive again; he was lost, and is found." And how did they respond? "They began to be merry" (Luke 15:24). This strong emotional element could not have occurred in a discourse about abstract ideas. We are not moved by such ideas. We are moved by people living out their lives in the concrete realities of our world. Tell about persons who were lost and found, who were sick and healed, who were separated and reunited, who were sinful and forgiven, and people will laugh with you and they will weep with you.

Fourth, be vivid in your preaching. Learn to use your imagination in the pulpit. Be picturesque in your speech. Give a visual quality to your ideas. Throw the great hopes, the great longings, and the great pain of your people upon the screens of their minds so they can be seen, and those who hear you will be moved.

In Revelation 22 which tells of the new life in the new city, we read: "They shall see his face," (v. 4). I can never read that without being moved. It speaks of something so deep in the human heart. We want our blurred vision made clear and our blindness healed so we can see God face to face. It is so simple and so vivid.

Emotion must never be used to manipulate people. This can so easily be done. It must come spontaneously from the life of the preacher, from the people who hear him, and from the gospel that is proclaimed.

THE WILL

Preaching appeals to the mind and the heart, but it makes its ultimate appeal to the will. You move for a verdict, for a decision. Christian truth is something you do, something you live.

Here is the essential difference between teaching and preaching. Teaching basically addresses the mind, while preaching, in the final analysis, is concerned with the will.

The preacher's business is not merely to discuss repentance but to persuade people to repent; not merely to discuss faith but to lead them to trust; not merely to discuss love but to appeal to them to be the love of Christ in our world. The preacher must never be content merely to present Christian truth in logical and cogent ways which can be clearly understood. Nor is his main task to stir deep feelings in his hearers which may be as short lived as the mist before the rising sun. The ultimate end of the sermon is to help the people embody the truth, give flesh and blood to it, and live it out in the concrete situations of life. His final appeal is to the will.

Jesus placed tremendous emphasis on the doing of the truth. "Not every one who says to me, 'Lord, Lord,'" he warned, "shall enter the kingdom of heaven, but he who does the will of my Father who is in heaven" (Matt. 7:21). "Lord, Lord" makes a good confession of faith, a good creed. But that is not enough. Only the doing of the Father's will suffices. "Lord, Lord" makes a good password, but what we must have is the *passdeed* which is doing God's will.

Jesus' conclusion of the Sermon on the mount began like this: "Every one then who hears these words of mine and does them will be like a wise man who built his house upon the rock" (Matt. 7:24). Hearing his words was not enough. There must be the doing of them.

Jesus declared that in the last judgment he would judge us not by our confessions and creeds but by our deeds of grace and mercy: Did we feed the hungry, give drink to the thirsty, take the stranger in, clothe the naked? Did we visit the sick and prisoners? These are the kinds of questions he will ask. The grace that saves us must become the gracious deed.

There are two kinds of appeals we make to the will in our

preaching: the first is the initial call to the Christian life which is evangelistic in nature. The other is to discipleship, to the growth and maturing of the believer in Christ.

The initial appeal to the will is not a call for faith that is essentially intellectual assent, nor trusting propositional truth. It is not a call to be a philosopher, who believes because the evidence tilts the intellectual scales toward God. It is a call to trust the grace and mercy seen in Christ. It is like a leap into the arms of God who is the Father of our Lord and Savior Jesus Christ. It is like a sailor who leaves his torpedoed ship and climbs into a lifeboat. We abandon our sinking style of life and get onto the grace that is in Christ. And as we make that radical act something of a radical nature happens to us: We are given a new relationship with God and a new life.

Beyond the initial call is the appeal to the discipline of discipleship. It becomes a nurturing and growing process, the end of which is "mature manhood, to the measure of the stature of the fullness of Christ" (Eph. 4:13). This involves a deep devotional life, a study of Scripture and doctrine, a vital identification with the church which is the community of faith, self-denial and sacrifice, ministry and service, a prophetic involvement with the world, and, above all, a growing life-style which has Christian love as its motivation.

Let us gather up what has been attempted in this chapter in a summary statement. The mind needs the heart to save it from being icy and cold. The will needs the heart, for only the heart can overcome the inertia, sluggishness, and timidity of the will. Only the heart can move the will to bold, daring, heroic, and sacrificial action.

But the heart needs the mind and the will. The mind can be a check on the heart. It can help keep the heart from overflowing its banks. It can be like a strong dike that holds back the floodwaters of the heart. And the heart needs the will. The will can help keep the power of the heart from evaporating and being lost. It can cut channels for the heart through which its vitality can flow into life and the world.

When you stand in the pulpit don't look at abstractions lifted from life. See faces. See persons and know that your overriding task is to address the whole gospel to the whole person. The years will reward you for this kind of faithfulness.

2
Creating Surprise in the Pulpit

One of the severe tragedies of Christian worship is: it is dull and boring for so many. It doesn't seem to matter greatly. They can take it or leave it. Nothing ever seems to happen. There are no surprises. When such is the case, preaching must take its full responsibility for this dullness and boredom.

We can't imagine New Testament worship being like that. We find a doxology of the early church in the first chapter of Revelation: "To him who loves us and has freed us from our sins by his blood and made us a kingdom, priests to his God and Father, to him be glory and dominion for ever and ever, Amen" (vv. 5-6). We can still feel the joyous and lilting quality of that worship. They rejoiced as those who had been in bondage and were then free. The manacles that had bound them had been broken. They had been delivered from the powers of darkness into the light of freedom which Christ gives. They had been saved from sinister powers, that hated them, into the love of God that could not give them up.

The preaching must have been just as exciting as that doxology. Their message was one of liberation and freedom. They remembered Israel's Exodus, and they told of a more recent and greater exodus that had occurred in Jesus Christ. In their own time God had performed the supremely liberating deed in Jesus Christ. In Christ they had been set free from the two ultimately enslaving realities—sin and death.

How do you infuse worship with wonder? How do you create surprise in the pulpit? A preacher could scarcely ask himself two more important questions than these.

FAITHFUL TO THE BIBLICAL MESSAGE

If we are going to create surprise in the pulpit, we have to be faithful and loyal to the biblical message.

The most surprising book in the world is the Bible. It is the story of God seeking us in love, finding us, and changing the human situation. We find wonder after wonder. We can't be faithful to the Bible, preaching it with imaginative power, and not create surprise.

The Bible can be thought of as a story in three episodes: God seeking the world through a special people, then through a special person, and finally through another special people. Each episode is full of surprises—many of them!

The first special people was Israel, who always stood in wonder of the fact that God ever called them. They lived their lives in surprise. Why God had called them was always a mystery. They were few in number, weak and vacillating, and often morally irresponsible and spiritually blind. Why them of all the people of earth? Deuteronomy raises this question: "The Lord your God has chosen you to be a people for his own possession, out of all the peoples that are on the face of the earth. It was not because you were more in number than any other people that the Lord set his love upon you and chose you, for you were the fewest of all peoples; but it is because the Lord loves you" (Deut. 7:6-8). Their being chosen lay in the mystery of God's love and grace.

Think of the surprising stories that grew out of the life of those special people. Think of Abraham and his family traveling westward, being powerfully moved by a strong spiritual impulse which gave him the sense of God's calling. Then came the night of nights when beneath a brilliant Syrian sky God said to him: "Look toward heaven, and number the stars, if you are able to number them. So shall your descendants be" (Gen. 15:5). He was without a son to carry on his line, and Sarah, his wife, was long past the childbearing period. How could it be? Abraham hoped against hope. And God's promise of a son was fulfilled when Sarah gave birth to Isaac. If that could be, anything could happen. Beyond that point, Abraham lived his life in surprise.

Jacob, a man fleeing from home for his life, slept beneath the stars in the wilderness with a stone for his pillow. It was an unlikely place to experience God. There were no altars, no chanting priests, no sacred Scriptures, no one preaching a sermon, no religious symbols, and no fellow pilgrims seeking God with him. Yet, there he was found by God. Jacob was surprised and was never able to outlive that mystery.

Who can forget Joseph who was sold into slavery by his own brothers. We would have expected the story to end there, but it didn't. The next time we hear of him he was in Egypt rising rapidly to lofty political power, not stopping until he was prime minister of that mighty land. Then, driven by famine, his brothers went to Egypt to buy grain. During a dramatic and poignant moment Joseph identified himself to his brothers, telling them not to blame themselves since God had sent him into Egypt. Imagine God overriding the inhuman cruelty of those brothers, being present in its pain and tragedy, and finally working out something wonderful and good from all of it. Surprised? Of course. There is no other word to tell it.

So throughout the Old Testament we see persons finding life more mysterious than they could imagine and events taking turns they could not anticipate. Surprise follows surprise.

Against the background of this special people, God sent a special person who was Jesus Christ, his Son. Jesus was born to Israel's race and was thoroughly steeped in her thought and faith. The element of surprise continued, being heightened.

The greatest surprise of all is the Incarnation. That the God of our universe should come to us in a frame as frail and fragile as a helpless baby, that he should take upon himself flesh—our kind of flesh that gets tired, that bleeds, and that dies—staggers the imagination. If people had considered before them the different ways God might have come to them, they would have chosen the Incarnation last of all. Then add to the mystery the fact that he to whom we sing coronation hymns was born, not in a palace but in a manger. The divine Son of God was born, not in the precinct of a temple but in one of the lowliest and most secular places imaginable.

Jesus Christ surprised people by the way he lived. His lifestyle was not what they expected. He turned the then current standard of greatness upside down. The great are those who serve, he taught, not those who exercise power and mastery. He refused a crown, and asked for a towel and basin of water. He did not seek wealth but espoused the life of poverty, not having a pillow whereon to lay his head. While open to all, he spent more of his time with the poor, the socially outcast, and sinners than with the rich, socially accepted, and religiously approved. He had a habit of associating with the "wrong kind of people." He was the friend of tax collectors and sinners, and ate with them. He was critical of the outward and popular forms of religion and told the religious leaders that they had "neglected the weightier matters of the law, justice and mercy and faith" (Matt. 23:23). He addressed in warm and intimate terms the God who was thought to be so far above our poor and tormented world that people would not call him by his personal name. Not only did he surprise people but he surprised them in a manner that threatened them. They reacted angrily and swore to do away with him.

The stories Jesus told usually turned out in unexpected ways. In his parable of the prodigal son, the reckless and profligate boy was the guest of honor at the banquet, while the dutiful and loyal son was a sulky, slinking figure who stood in the shadows of the banquet hall, refusing to go in despite the fact his father had greatly entreated him. We would not have expected it to end like that.

Or take Jesus' parable of the laborers in the vineyard. Some had worked twelve hours, some nine, some six, some three, and some one. But at the close of day, they were all paid the same. The ones who had worked only one hour received as much as those who had worked twelve, toiling through the heat of the day. That didn't seem right.

The two most significant events in the life of Jesus, his death and resurrection, were the biggest of surprises. Who expected the Messiah of God to be put to death on a shameful Roman cross? Nobody did, not even those closest to him, although Jesus had told them he must go to Jerusalem and be put to death. But to add wonder to wonder, the early church looked back on that event and saw it do God's marvelous redemptive deed. That is how God saves people. It is little wonder the world was shocked by it. Jews were offended, while Greeks saw it as foolishness.

Then came Easter morning. Who had expected the resurrection? No one, not even Jesus' disciples with whom he had shared the hope. When the women who were first at the empty tomb told the apostles, those who should have found it easiest to believe received the news as "an idle tale," (Luke 24:11) which in medical terms was wild talk of persons in delirium or hysteria. They thought the women were hallucinating, hearing and seeing things that did not exist, except in their sick minds. And when they had the evidence in the person of the risen Lord with his torn hands and wounded side, the surprise did not go away. They knew they were in the presence of mystery.

The element of surprise does not pass with the coming of another special people which is the new Israel or the church. The new Israel was as baffled as the old one as to why God chose them. For the most part the church was composed of poor and obscure people. Paul reminded the Corinthian church that not many of their members were wise according to worldly standards, not many were powerful, not many were of noble birth. Why had not God chosen more prominent and powerful people to do his work?

Yet, the church was surprised when they remembered who they had been and acknowledged who they were now. You feel wonder in Peter's words: "But you are a chosen race, a royal priesthood, a holy nation, God's own people, that you may declare the wonderful deeds of him who called you out of darkness into his marvelous light. Once you were no people but now you are God's people; once you had not received mercy but now you have received mercy" (1 Pet. 2:9-10). The church wondered at the power of its gospel. "It is the power of God for salvation," Paul wrote, "to every one who has faith" (Rom. 1:16). It was the dynamite of God, blasting the stronghold of evil powers and setting captives free. The church was amazed at the power given it in the presence of the Holy Spirit. The Holy Spirit found them weak and vacillating and made them indomitably strong. The church stood in awe of the melting down of barriers as the gospel was preached, and in the midst of it all was an amazing miracle—Jew and Gentile, so antagonistic and far apart, were becoming one, a new humanity within the church. Those who wrote the New Testament were astonished at the versatility and many-faceted reality of the church. Many metaphors are used to describe it. Paul's favorite term for the church was the body of Christ. That is a truth our minds cannot fathom, but Paul must have meant that in some real sense the Incarnation was continued in the church. Christ wanted to continue his life in the world through the church which is his body. That is mystery enough.

That element of surprise is projected beyond history. Christian faith envisions a new heaven and a new earth. There will be a radically new kind of life in a new order. There will be an eternal city, the new Jerusalem, in which there will not be a trace of evil or pain. There will be no sorrow, no tears, and no death. Some of the most extravagant language of the world's literature is used to tell of the magnificence of that city and the glory of the life that will be in it. It all defies human imagination.

RECAPTURING THE SURPRISE

We may intellectually accept the reality of surprise in the biblical message, yet not be able to recapture it in our preaching. Our preaching may seem lifeless to us and those who hear us. We may feel that our preaching bores people.

What will enable us to recapture this strange quality of surprise in the biblical message? Let me suggest four things: Approach the Bible historically, interpret it theologically, enter it imaginatively, and let the Holy Spirit cast its light upon it.

The Bible has come to us out of our history. God meets us and saves us along our different paths. God discloses himself in historical events and historical persons, especially one, Jesus of Nazareth. Some people fear the historical approach to Scripture but we should not be afraid. We should be grateful since it is one of the finest gifts of biblical scholarship. This approach is one of the keys that unlocks the Scriptures, and without it we cannot go in. We can never recover the freshness of the biblical message unless we come at it historically. When we do, it is surprising what new meanings passages have that once seemed dull and lifeless.

Take, for example, Jesus' parable of the good Samaritan. We can't feel the jolt of surprise unless we know how despised the Samaritan was in Jewish society. He belonged to a hybrid race, was hated, and totally rejected by the Jews. Understandng that, we know what risky business it was for Jesus to tell a story where the hero was a Samaritan. Who would have expected a despised Samaritan to have shown compassion on the robbed and wounded man? And who would have expected a Samaritan to have been more acceptable to God than a priest and Levite who served God in one of the most sacred places in Jewish life, the Temple at Jerusalem? Is it any wonder the people saw Jesus as a dangerous radical?

But the historical approach is not sufficient within itself. It is not enough to know dates, places, persons, and events, as helpful as these are. We have to interpret the Bible theologically; that is, we need to be able to trace God's presence and action in those historical places, persons, and events. What makes the Bible a unique book is that God is seen as being present, acting, judging, and redeeming in the historical events it records. We miss, for example, the deep meaning of the Exodus unless we see God present, liberating helpless slaves. We cannot understand the Christ event unless we see God uniquely present in the birth, life, death, and resurrection of Jesus.

Also, we need to approach the bible imaginatively. Imagination helps you to enter those redemptive situations in some real sense, to be present at the crossing of the Red Sea, to go with the shepherds to the manger in Bethlehem, to walk with Jesus and his disciples along the roads of Galilee, to stand near the cross where Jesus was crucified, and to visit the empty tomb with those women on that first Easter morning. Such imagination has almost magical power.

J. H. Jowett called it historical imagination without which, he thought, there is unreality about our preaching. "If we do not realize the past," he wrote, "we cannot get its vital message for the present. The past which unfolded in the pages of Scripture is to many of us very wooden; we do not feel their breathing; we do not hear them cry; we do not hear them laugh; we do not mix with their humanness and find they are just like folk in the next street. And so the message is not alive." Jowett goes on to state that a preacher should study the Scripture historically and enter it imaginatively so the world of the Bible "becomes so vivid that you can scarcely tell whether you are a preacher in your study, or a citizen in some village, or city, or empire of the past."[1]

Finally, we need the Holy Spirit to illumine and empower the biblical truth we preach. God has revealed himself in human history, but people could not trace God's plan in their own efforts. They needed help and found it in the Holy Spirit. The Holy Spirit was like a flare dropped upon the dark landscape of history, lighting up its contours so men and women could see God's presence and action there.

In our preaching, we still need the Holy Spirit shedding his light upon the truth we speak. For only then can we see and understand its deep spiritual dimensions. We should constantly keep in mind the words of Jesus: "When the Spirit of truth comes, he will guide you into all the truth" (John 16:13).

FELT IN THE PREACHER

Let the element of surprise be seen and felt in the life of the preacher.

The personal element is important in preaching. The preacher is no nonentity standing in the pulpit. He is a person, hopefully a person who has encountered God in Christ. He should be a person who has been surprised by the amazing grace of Christ. Unless he has, he will be slow to find the surprising element in the gospel he preaches.

When Saul of Tarsus was converted, everybody was surprised. Judaism was surprised that its leading theological star had defected, joining the ranks of the enemy. Christians were surprised. Ananias, one of their leaders in Damascus, was surprised. When he was commanded by the Lord to seek out Saul of Tarsus in Judas' house on Straight Street, he protested: "Lord, I have heard from many about this man how much evil he has done to thy saints in Jerusalem; and here he has authority from the chief priests to bind all who call upon thy name" (Acts 9:13). It all seemed so impossible. But it was possible. It was true. Saul, the fierce enemy of the church, had become a Christian.

But no one was more surprised than Saul himself. How could it be? How was it that he now called Lord one whom he had cursed and despised? How was it that he suddenly did an about-face, rejecting that which he once loved and loving now that which he once hated? How was it that God had accepted him in grace without any moral requirements at all? How was it that faith in Jesus Christ was enough for God to declare him righteous before him? How was it his restless and tormented soul found rest for the first time by simply believing in Jesus Christ? He couldn't understand, but one thing was sure: It had really happened.

Paul continued to live in the wonder of it all. He told how Christ appeared to him "as one untimely born" (1 Cor. 15:8). He felt himself unfit to be an apostle since he had persecuted the church of God. He once testified: "But by the grace of God I am what I am" (1 Cor. 15:10). He didn't become what he was by moral striving and spiritual discipline. He had nothing to offer God. His new life was a gift of grace.

Again Paul wrote: "This is a faithful saying, and worthy of all acceptation, that Christ Jesus came into the world to save sinners, of whom I am chief" (1 Tim. 1:15, KJV). If Christ could save Paul, he could save anybody. Paul had been the chief of sinners. This was reason enough for him to live his life in surprise.

You may not have had an experience of salvation as dramatic as that of Paul. You may not be able to name the place, day, and hour. Yours may have been much less dramatic, but the experience of God's grace in your life should be equally as real.

It may have been like the coming of spring. When did winter pass into spring? We can't be sure. There was, of course, the official day of spring, but it may have been cold and blustery, more like winter than spring. While spring came officially that day, it did not actually come. But when the days are warm and balmy, when the landscape is green with life, when trees put forth their leaves, flowers bloom, and birds sing, we know that spring has come. We can't be sure when, but that it has come there can be no doubt. God's grace in our lives may be like the coming of spring. Because it was more gradual, and not so sudden and dramatic, does not mean it is any less real.

The grace that forgives our sins, sets our lives right with God, and gives us new life is the same grace that puts the word of hope in our hearts and the good news of the gospel on our lips. It is surprising indeed that God should call us to be his spokesmen.

Whether women should be ordained to the ministry is a bone of contention in many denominations. Yet, I had a bright young woman as a student who was an excellent and gifted preacher. Her way into the ministry was rather circuitous, and one day she told us about her pilgrimage. She had attended a well-known university for her undergraduate work, and was then graduated from the law school of that university. She became a member of a prestigious law firm and did some teaching at the law school of which she was a graduate. She was obviously most successful, yet she remained restless and unfulfilled. She took a course in clinical pastoral education, and discovered how wonderful it was to relate the love and hope of the Christian gospel to sick people. For the first time she felt fulfilment on some deep level. From that experience she went into the ministry. She summarized her long pilgrimage like this: "Surprised by grace!" The class knew she would continue to be surprised as a minister of Christ.

GOD'S ACTION IN OUR WORLD

It is not enough to point to God's action in the past. We need to be surprised by him in our contemporary world. We must trace his steps across the landscape of our modern history. The God who has acted, acts again; the God who has spoken, speaks again, the God who has liberated, liberates again, the God who has saved, saves again; the God who has been with his people, is with them again.

Lives are still being changed and the human situation redeemed by the grace of Christ. God is not locked in the past. He is still present and active in his world. He is not dead nor does he sleep. The wonders of his grace are as real now as ever.

One of the interesting features of the *Good News Bible* is that truths are illustrated with simple sketches by Annie Vallaton, as for example Romans 6:6: "And we know that our old being has been put to death with Christ on his cross, in order that the power of the sinful self might be destroyed, so that we should no longer be the slaves of sin." The illustration pictures a man approaching the cross of Jesus bearing a crushing load of guilt. He is indeed a slave of sin. He drops his heavy load at the foot of the cross and moves beyond it as a free man.

Robert G. Bratcher, the basic translator of this translation of the New Testament, told about a copy of it falling into the hands of a prisoner in Australia. The inmate turned to the illustration of Romans 6:6, studied it for a moment, and said: "I am that man." He did what that man did. He dropped his terrible load of guilt and shame at the foot of the cross of Christ, accepted the gift of forgiveness, and went away a free man.

Commander Mitsuo Fuchida led the Japanese air attack on Pearl Harbor, signaling the doom of thousands of Americans. After the war, Fuchida, upon hearing falsely that the Americans were torturing their Japanese prisoners, became more bitter than ever against the Americans for dropping the atomic bomb on Hiroshima and Nagasaki. In searching for evidence to confirm the atrocities of Americans against his own people, he talked with a friend who had been imprisoned in a hospital in Utah, asking him what he thought. The friend told about a nurse whose parents were missionaries and had been murdered by the Japanese in the Philippines. Yet, she had nursed injured Japanese soldiers back to health with love and kindness. This story deeply moved Fuchida and while he was still shaken up, he was given a tract which told about an American bombardier who had been captured and tortured by the Japanese in a prison camp. One day a Japanese guard gave the bombardier a Bible. The American, who violently hated his captors, read about Christ's love and redemption. When be believed in Christ, his hate was changed to love.

About that time a Japanese translation of the Bible fell into Fuchida's hands. In Luke 23 he read about Christ's prayer just before he died. "I met Jesus that day," Fuchida said. "He came into my heart and changed my life from a military officer to a warrior for Christ." He turned down the highest position in the Japanese Air Force so he could preach the gospel of Christ.

We have been talking about dramatic examples of God's grace in people's lives. Many, many people, however, live their lives each day in less spectacular ways, and yet bring high courage to life where they face overwhelming odds, make pain and handicaps creative, and absorb the anger and bitterness of people without striking back. But how? Christ says to them what he said to Paul, "My grace is sufficient for you, for my strength is made perfect in weakness" (2 Cor. 12:9).

We must trace God's redemptive action, not only in individual lives but on history's larger scale. Africa is a good example of this.

At the beginning of this century only four percent of Africa was Christian. Missionaries continued to trickle in, founding churches, schools, hospitals, and model farms, and through all of it holding out the hope of the Christian gospel. These efforts received a very generous response. It is now estimated that 46 percent of Africa will be Christian when the twenty-first century begins. When this estimate was first made some fifteen years ago, it seemed more like wishful thinking than reality. Some professors of Christian missions were consulted. They all agreed that, while there were variables to be reckoned with, it was possible. Africa has been considered a mission field during the twentieth century, but it will certainly be one of the strong bases of missionary advance during the twenty-first. Who at the beginning of this century would have thought in such staggering terms? In our time this prospect is one of those great surprises on a wide historical scale.

It is too bad when people come to Christian worship, carrying no sense of expectancy. To find the gospel of Jesus Christ dull and boring is to miss the good news of God's redemptive action in Jesus Christ. We are to preach the liberating action of God, especially his mighty deed in Jesus Christ, and we are to worship as those who have been set free. When that happens, we will be surprised. And who, more than anyone else, is the key to surprise? The preacher. If he doesn't stand amazed in the wonder of God's grace, should he think it strange if his people do not?

3
Achieving Clarity in the Pulpit

A few summers ago I worshiped at the Waikiki Baptist Church in Honolulu, Hawaii. The associate pastor preached that morning, and before he began his sermon he said: "Not all of you will agree with me this morning, but I want to make sure that all of you understand what I say." And they did. A child could not have missed his message.

He began by saying that often Paul drew metaphors from athletics. This helped make his message fresh and understandable. He said he was going to do that. He would compare the Christian life to a baseball diamond: First base is accepting Christ, second base is baptism and church membership, third base is Christian service, and home plate is heaven and eternal life. He closed his sermon rather dramatically by telling about an incident that occurred in the World Series of 1925. It was the ninth inning and the score was tied. It was an exciting moment when a player hit a home run. Quickly he ran the bases. The spectators rose to their feet, clapping and cheering. Then a most unexpected thing happened: The umpire called the runner out. The huge crowd was angry and dismayed. "Why?" they were asking. The runner had not touched first base. Then the preacher said, "If you don't touch first base, you can't reach heaven." The sermon was at an end.

Preaching is, at its heart, communication. But communication will be ineffective unless clarity is achieved in the pulpit. Rudolph Flesch in his book, *The Art of Plain Talk,* has written: "There is nothing more important to you as a speaker and writer than that your audience understands you." That is certainly true of the preacher in the pulpit.

No one else has the responsibility to communicate as clearly as does the preacher. He more than anyone else is dealing with issues as crucial as life and death. He has a word of life to speak to men and women caught in the grip of death. He dare not be inarticulate!

One powerful preacher of the past said he prayed a silent prayer before he preached: "O God, some one person here needs what I am going to say. Help me to reach him." That is a prayer every preacher should pray, and in part it is a prayer for clarity.

What will enable the preacher to achieve clarity in the pulpit?

OWN IDEAS CLEARLY DEFINED

The preacher must make sure that his own ideas are clearly and accurately defined.

One is afraid that this is not always the case. We may suspect that there is a lot of sloppy thinking in the pulpit; that often ideas are hazy, fuzzy, and poorly defined. We wonder what would happen in many cases if a bright layman should stand up and challenge his pastor. "Now what do you mean by that term?" We are afraid that often there would be a long, embarrassing period of silence, then some stammering, and finally the confession: "I am not sure what I mean." Unless a preacher has clearly defined his own ideas, there is no way of communicating with clarity.

There are several things that will help the preacher to define clearly his own ideas. There is, of course, no substitute for serious and disciplined study. He should study the Bible systematically and should saturate his mind with great biblical themes. He should have excellent commentaries, as well as other tools for scholarly study. Also, it is a good discipline to write your sermons. If you can write your sermon, you know you have achieved some clarity of thought.

Special attention should be given to theological ideas and terms. Theology, like any discipline, has its own technical language. We can, therefore, not escape theological terminology in the pulpit. But translating theological concepts into ideas, and theological language into terms that laymen can understand, is one of the greatest challenges a preacher faces. Laymen often feel that theological ideas are abstract and far removed from practical living and that theological language is difficult to understand. It is the task of the preacher to show how theology impinges on life at its most crucial points, that theology is living and relevant, and that theological terms are understandable.

How do you go about making theological truth clear? To me there are four steps. *First, know the meaning of theological terms, their historical development, and their etymology.* You will often make an interesting discovery: Theological terms were usually secular before they were religious. They were normally lifted from the living experience of the common life. When one discovers this, one has taken a step toward understanding that theological language was never intended to be difficult and strange. A lexicon and biblical dictionary are good tools.

Again, know the historical background of the theological idea. How did it originate and what was its earliest meaning? For example, the theological concept of redemption was suggested by slavery. It came from common and contemporary life since slavery pervaded the ancient world. When a slave was set free, he was redeemed. The basic meaning of the term was freedom or liberation.

Further, draw upon modern life to shed additional light on the concept. Lay beside it a parallel from the contemporary situation. For example, *Time* magazine captioned its story of our returning Vietnam POWs, "The Celebration of Men Redeemed." Here was a secular magazine resorting to religious language in telling one of the great stories of the decade. "Celebration" and "redeemed" are basically religious terms. Our prisoners of war had been redeemed in that they had been liberated from their captors. They were now free. They had been held by an alien power, but now they could return to the country and the people to whom they belonged.

Finally, show the meaning of the term and concept for our contemporary life with its needs and hopes. Let us pursue the meaning of redemption. It is true that we are not political slaves, but we understand what it is to be in bondage to dark and evil powers. Who does not know what it is to be caught, trapped, hemmed in, imprisoned, enslaved? When the bonds that bind us are snapped, when the chains that hold us are struck, when the bars that imprison are borne away, we are redeemed. We are set free from the powers that do no care for us, that would enslave us, and finally destroy us.

WITHIN RANGE OF EXPERIENCE

Ideas and language must fall within the experience of those who hear; else, they will not understand what we say. Our ideas will be mysterious and elusive.

This does not mean that we are the source of our gospel. We indeed are not. While the gospel should pass through our experience, it does not originate with us. The gospel we experience can be like light shining through a stained-glass window. While the glass is not impervious to the light, it cannot be the source of it. Its source is the heavens, yet when passing through the window it takes on the rich qualities of the stained glass. The gospel we preach has its source in God and his mighty action. While clothing it with our own words, the word we speak is God's. He has spoken—therefore we speak.

One of the wonders of the gospel is that we can express it through our thought forms and in our language. This is possible for several reasons. *First, God has acted in our history and therefore his action can be expressed in our thoughts and words.* The Exodus of the Old Testament didn't happen in the heavens, in some ethereal realm where divinities were set free from bondage. No, it happened in human history, in a particular human history—Israel's. So, Israel could tell about it. It was something that had happened to them. Hosea heard God saying: "When Israel was a child, I loved him, and out of Egypt I called my son" (Hos. 11:1). It was so basically human and historical that a child could understand it. Israel could sing about their great deliverance: "The sea looked and fled, Jordan turned back. The mountains skipped like rams, and the hills like lambs" (Ps. 114:3-4). They could talk and sing about the great event because it had fallen within their range of experience.

Again, when God got ready to address us in most un-mistakable terms, he did it through a person who spoke our language, walked in our common ways, knew our weariness and fatigue, our joy and our pain, who underwent our temptations, and died our death. Jesus, while being the Son of God, was thoroughly historical and human. In some real sense he was one of us. His life was lived within the broad range of our human experience. You can talk about a person like that.

Finally, the gospel we preach is a word about us, for us, and to us. When the word we preach does not reach people it is like an arrow deflected from its course, therefore missing its target. Its target is a human one. The Incarnation tells us that Jesus Christ came into the midst of our existence, where we live, struggle, hope, and die. The Christmas angel announced: "For to you is born this day in the city of David a Savior, who is Christ the Lord" (Luke 2:12). Nothing ethereal and faraway about that. It is "to you" the Savior has come, and he has been born "in the city of David" (v. 11). Where is this city of David? Just over the way. It is close by. Nothing can be more in touch with our lives than the gospel we preach.

In looking for somebody whose message fell within the range of their hearers' experience, we could not find two better examples than Jesus and Paul.

Jesus was more a layman than a priest. He never was ordained. His language was more secular than religious. He used language laymen understood. He talked about sunsets being red and dawns being lowering. He spoke of farmers, shepherds, craftsmen, and merchants. He talked about women patching old garments the fabric of which was so bare that it could not take patch of new cloth. He never discussed truth abstractly. He told stories everyone could understand. When he talked about the terrible tragedy of human existence, he didn't discuss it abstractly. Rather, he told about a lost sheep, a lost coin, and a lost son. When speaking about the kingdom of God, he told about a mustard seed, leaven hidden in three measures of flour, a treasure buried in a field, a merchant seeking fine pearls, and a net cast into the sea.

Paul, like Jesus, used language understood by his world. His terminology was taken fresh from the life of people. For most part, though not always, it came from the secular parlance of his time. He gave religious meaning to secular speech and ideas, and these have passed over into our technical theological vocabulary. For example, his term *justification* came from the courts, *reconciliation* from the common estrangements of life, *adoption* from the family and courts, and *redemption,* as already suggested, from slavery. The terms *propitiation* (expiation) came from then current religion and people understood their meaning. Paul was careful not to use difficult and esoteric speech. He deliberately used familiar language so he could speak clearly and forcefully. He had the deepest conviction that he had a message without which people could not really live. But why speak about it if people could not understand him?

Jesus and Paul spoke in such a way that their truth fell within the range of the experience of the people who heard them and in language they could understand—but can we? Yes, if we are willing to stay in touch with our people and with our gospel. When we are aware of loneliness, separation, estrangement, anxiety, frustration, anonymity, the feeling of helplessness before overwhelming forces, the experience of being trapped and hemmed in, guilt and shame both in our personal and corporate life, meaninglessness, the mystery of pain and death, we can. When we speak of these experiences, we are dealing with the hallmarks of modern life. Our gospel is at home with these experiences. It was addressed to them, and can speak redemptively to them now. But what about theological language? If we are willing to define it, amplify it in terms of current experience, and draw parallels between the historical situation (that created the language) and modern life, we will discover that our most technical terms can be fresh and have strange powers of communication.

LANGUAGE THAT IS CONCRETE

We should use language that is concrete, vivid, picturesque, and down-to-earth.

I have long felt that pulpit language is often too abstract, spiritual, ethereal, heavenly, and pretty. Several years ago I was speaking to some ministers about pulpit language. I said I thought it should have an earthly quality about it, and some of the ministers were offended. They thought I meant it should be crude and vulgar. I of course didn't mean that at all. I simply meant that it should reflect the common realities of the life we live.

Someone has said that it is body language that best communicates. That offends some of us because we still have a docetism that will not allow us to accept our bodies fully and freely. They are not spiritual enough. We should remember, however, that when God looked out upon his creation, which included human bodies, he pronounced it very good. An expression of the face, a glance of the eyes, an emotional quality of the voice, use of the hands, and the posture of the body can be powerful communicators. We must not forget that we are sensate creatures. That is what makes sensory language so important.

Dwight E. Stevenson has written: "In a word, a living sermon goes back to the grass roots of human experience—not to concepts, but to precepts; not to words, but to things."[1] When we get back to grass roots of human experience, we get back to sensory experience. Our earliest experiences came through our five senses, and our five senses continue to be basic media of experiencing our world, people, and even ideas. That is why sensory language has such great power to communicate. It is important that language in the pulpit appeal to seeing, touch, hearing, and even tasting and smelling. It is especially important that language appeal to the eye. Ideas that have visual power are especially effective. There is an Arab proverb which says: "He is the best speaker who can turn ears into eyes."

It would be a good discipline for any pastor, having written his sermon for Sunday, to go over it carefully and indicate in the margins where ideas are visual. If he is unable to make such notations, he should write his sermon over again, using metaphors and images that give visual power to his ideas.

We keep coming back to our earliest experiences. A man may speak a dozen languages, but in some great pain or tragedy or in dying he will cry out in his native tongue. In our best communication, we use language that grows out of our earliest experience which is sensory.

It is extremely important to observe that this is the kind of language the Bible frequently uses. It does not use abstract terms. Its language is concrete, earthly, sensory. Let us take some examples. "Consider the lilies of the field, how they grow;

they neither toil, nor spin; yet I tell you, even Solomon in all his glory was not arrayed like one of these" (Matt. 6:28-29). That appeals to the eye. "His voice was like the sound of many waters" (Rev 1:15). That appeals to the ear. "Behold, I have put my words in your mouth" (Jer. 1:9). That appeals to touch. "O taste and see that the Lord is good!" (Ps. 34:8). That appeals to taste. "Instead of perfume there will be rottenness" (Isa. 3:24). That appeals to smell.

The Bible is so rich in sensory images that a combination will often occur in a single verse. Seeing and hearing: "Let the floods clap their hands; let the hills sing for joy together" (Ps. 98:8). Hearing, seeing, and touching: "That which was from the beginning, which we have heard, which we have seen with our eyes, which we looked upon and touched with our hands, concerning the word of life" (1 John 1:1).

We should not think because a spiritual truth is clothed in sensory image that it is any less spiritual. Such language allows spiritual truth to speak vividly and concretely to us. We have the supreme example in the way the New Testament talks about the Incarnation: "The Word was made flesh, and dwelt among us" (John 1:14, KJV). It could not have been more earthly. Was Christ less spiritual because he had a body? Of course not.

There is a word of caution. We should not rule out abstract language, even in the pulpit. Some truths are best expressed in abstract terms, and to express them in any other manner would do violence to the truth. But abstract speech in the pulpit should be used sparingly.

Now let us emphasize style before we move on. The written, as well as the oral style, has a very close relationship with the language we use. Style should have clarity, vividness, force, beauty, as well as other qualities. The style of a sermon should be more akin to poetry than to any other literary form. It should be rich in metaphors, similes, imagery, word pictures, and analogies.

No minister should minimize style. A magnificent truth is often lost because the style is poor, while a mediocre truth may survive, becoming popular, because the style is good. We will write more about style in a later chapter.

USE IMAGINATION

Use imagination responsibly. It is one of our finest gifts.

There are few things in preaching fraught with such dangers and possibilities as the use of imagination. Imagination is one of the most wonderful of all human faculties. Therefore, it should be used in preaching. Imagination can take an old truth, touch it to life, giving it freshness and power. An unimaginative and prosaic mind in the pulpit may leave the Bible a record of an ancient past with strange customs and lifeless forms, whereas the Bible is meant to be a book throbbing with life and vitality, whose old truths are transposable into the living present. Imagination has immense power to make the Bible come alive.

Yet, imagination used irresponsibly can be very dangerous. It can distort the truth, rob the preacher of integrity, and caricature reality. The principle of using imagination responsibly is simple to keep it in touch with reality and make it the servant of truth.

Imagination, more than anything else, can make biblical truth vivid and in some cases more understandable. It is part of the answer to the problem of technical theological concepts and language to which reference has already been made. To illustrate, let us return to the idea of redemption. A preacher wanting to make that truth come alive told an imaginary story about Paul. He introduced the story by saying that Paul lived in a world of slavery. He saw slaves wherever he went and often counted them among his best friends, as he did Onesimus. One day Paul was passing a slave market where a young man was being auctioned to the highest bidder. The young man and his family had been taken as spoils of war and had been carried from their country as slaves. Obviously, this young man was no ordinary human being. He was tall, strong, and aristocratic in bearing. He looked intelligent and the marks of culture were on him. He must have come from a privileged family. When purchased, he could easily be the finest, best educated, and most capable member of the family. Paul thought, *What a shame and an indignity for that young man to be a slave.* He was sorry that such a fate had overtaken him. The bidding began. Paul observed a gentle, soft-spoken man on the outskirts of the crowd who consistently topped the highest bid, finally bidding him in. What would he do with this young man? Paul was very curious, and as the man and his newly acquired slave moved away from the crowd, Paul followed close enough to hear their conversation. The purchaser said to the young man: "I have redeemed you. I bought you that I might liberate you. You are no longer a slave. You are a free man."

Out of that imaginary story the congregation came to a clearer understanding of redemption than they had had before. After the service a man, who was reputed to be the best Bible student in the church, asked: "Where do you find that story in the New Testament?" The preacher had to confess that it was not in the New Testament. Yet, it was legitimate. It was in touch with reality. The story told it the way it was, and the story was the servant of a wonderful truth: God in Christ has freed us from the bondage of sin and liberated us from the ultimate tragedy of death.

Characters of the Bible who may be more like shadowy figures than real flesh and blood people can come strangely alive under the touch of imagination. They can walk with us, talk with us, live with us, ask the questions we ask, and often give the answers we are searching for.

Frederick Buechner excels in this kind of approach. He uses imagery born of imagination. With a few words he can turn an ancient biblical character into a contemporary figure as for example: "Zacchaeus climbs up in a sycamore tree a crook and climbs down a saint. Paul sets out a hatchet man for the Pharisees and comes back a fool for Christ." He describes Abraham and Sarah's reaction to the news that Sarah, now long past her childbearing period, is going to have a son, like this: "The old woman's name is Sarah, of course, and the old man's name is Abraham, and they are laughing at the idea of a baby's being born in the geriatric ward and Medicare's picking up the tab."[2]

We are living through a time when the level of intelligence of congregations to whom we will preach is rising and when our people will have a growing impatience with poor preaching. In their world, where things are made clear through visual media and where they read well-written articles which clearly present ideas, they will increasingly reject fuzzy and obscure ideas of the pulpit. It is almost as if the effort at clarity is being forced on us. But there is a more basic reason why we should strive for clear articulation: We have a word to speak without which people perish. Therefore, a preacher who doesn't strive for this should examine his motives. Why is he in the pulpit anyway?

4
Cultivating Style in the Pulpit

The word *style* comes from *stylus* which was a pointed iron instrument used by Romans in writing on tablets covered with wax. It later came to mean a person's style of writing, and was expanded more broadly to include one's manner of thought, either in writing or in speech.

It is important to give attention to style, to cultivate it as an art, since a sermon is remembered more by its style than its content. That is sad, but it is true. Many a good sermon is forgotten because the style is bad, while many a bad sermon is remembered because the style is good.

John A. Broadus, who was a master homiletician, wrote: "Style is the glitter and polish of the warrior's sword, but is also the keen edge. It can make mediocrity acceptable and even attractive, a power more powerful still. It can make error seductive while truth may be unnoticed for lack of it."[1]

Chrysostom, whose name means "golden-mouthed," is considered by many scholars to be the greatest preacher in the history of the Christian movement. Ancient sermons are very difficult to read, but those of Chrysostom are notable exceptions. This does not mean that his content was better than some of the preachers of his day. Then why more easily read? His style, he had fine descriptive abilities. Scarcely a page of his sermons goes without some allusion or illustration.

A television consultant says that style is 90 percent responsible for the effectiveness of television communication while content is responsible for only 10 percent.

If you want your sermon easily heard, easily read, and easily remembered, give attention to style. It is of utmost importance.

MORE LIKE POETRY

We repeat that preaching is very much akin to poetry. It is more like poetry than prose, essay, scientific, or any other literary form. It should be rich in metaphor, simile, imagery, and analogy.

D. W. Cleverly Ford has reminded us that the form proper to preaching is poetic. "God is not a thing," he writes. "God is not something which can be caught in a net, extracted, examined, measured, weighed, and analyzed into its component parts. The scientific approach does not, therefore, obtain in this field of study. God is at least personal, and has all the mystery of the personal and more. And wherever description or interpretation of existence from the angle of the personal is undertaken, a form of expression has to be adopted which brings reality it touches closer by means of feeling, using word pictures, metaphors, similes, and imperfect analogies."[2]

Frederick Buechner has reminded us that the language the prophets used is essentially the "language of poetry, which more than polemics or philosophy, logic or theology, is the language of truth."[3] The same is true of the gospel and preaching. This is so "because truth in the sense of fullness, of the way things are, can best be pointed to by language of poetry-of metaphor, image, symbol."[4]

It becomes clear why the poetic form is best for preaching. Poetry, like preaching, seeks to see truth in its wholeness. It does not analyze and dissect truth. It may in fact be able to behold only a facet of truth but it does not dismantle truth. It may touch only the hem of the robe of truth but it does not dissect the robe.

Poetry, better than science, can speak of personhood and the relation of persons. There is without doubt great value in scientific tests, experiments, and evaluations of the human mind and personality. Let it be said that we have learned much from this approach and that we are much in debt to science. But in this method, personhood becomes an object. The real meaning and mystery of personhood elude this approach. It is only when a person is subject, not object, and when relationships of mutuality, love, and truth have been entered upon between persons, that we learn the real meaning of personhood. Here is the principal concern of preaching. It tells of a God who has disclosed his personhood and who wants to enter into a saving and loving relationship with his children. Preaching mediates between a loving God and people. God seeks a loving response from persons and wants them to enter into caring and loving relationships with one another. Preaching is basically concerned with the person of Jesus Christ who makes all of these relationships possible.

Poetry addresses truth to the whole person. It appeals not only to the mind but to the heart, will, and imagination. Truth is not only to be thought. It is to be felt and it is to be lived. Poetry goes further. It appeals to the sensory nature—seeing, hearing, touching, tasting, and smelling. It never apologizes for our sensory nature. It never sees persons as being dichotomous. It sees them in their wholeness. This is why its symbolism, simile, metaphor, and imagery are so important. Only these can represent truth to the whole person.

It goes without saying that preaching is concerned with the wholeness of truth and the wholeness of persons—and in the bringing of these together. It addresses the gospel to the whole person. Christian truth is to be grasped by the mind, experienced by the heart, and lived by the will. Preaching, like poetry, does not see man as a dichotomous creature. He is one and he is whole; therefore, preaching does not envision salvation exclusively in spiritual terms. The whole life is to be saved. Even the body is to be redeemed. It is little wonder preaching best conveys its message in poetic form.

While science seeks to scatter mystery with the light of reason, poetry knows that there is mystery beyond the reach of rational powers. This, however, does not mean that poetry is necessarily infused with Christian faith. Philosophically it may be naturalistic and humanistic. But even then, it knows there are boundaries beyond which the mind cannot go. Only the heart and imagination can cross them.

Preaching is concerned with authentic wonder and mystery which are the springs of prayer and worship. The mind quickly reaches frontiers of mystery beyond which it cannot pass. What comes from beyond those frontiers must be gift, must be revelation. Preaching knows the gift and helps speak of it.

MARKS OF GOOD STYLE

While the basic style of preaching is related to poetry, let us be more specific and talk about the marks of good style.

John A. Broadus who wrote a textbook, *On the Preparation and Delivery of Sermons,* more widely used than any other text in the history of preaching, said that style should include clarity, force, and beauty with clarity being the most important of the three.

Charles R. Brown, the superb teacher of preaching at Yale Divinity School, said that a sermon should have clearness, force, and natural beauty.

Paul Scherer in his Lyman Beecher Lectures revealed four principles of style: Truthful words with no exaggeration, simple words, picturesque words, and words that give clarity.

All three of these masters of the pulpit said essentially the same thing.

Here I dare to suggest seven qualities of good style.

First, clarity. Broadus wrote that it is first, and I believe it is.

We sometimes think that profound things cannot be clear and that clear things cannot be profound. That is a dreadful mistake. Sometimes that which seems profound is nothing more than a cover-up for the inability to be clear.

Jesus is proof that profound things can be clear. Jesus talked about the gigantic issues of life with such clarity.

I have always considered it a supreme compliment when a mother during the week would tell me: "Johnnie understood what you said Sunday morning. He has been talking and asking questions about it." I appreciated that much more than some self-styled sophisticate saying, "You certainly were profound this morning."

How does one achieve clarity? Move through your own muddled thinking until your ideas are clear. This is one of the reasons that writing a sermon is so important. You have to achieve some kind of clarity with an idea before you can put it down on paper. Also, it is good to test your ideas on a child or an adult of average intelligence. If your ideas are clear to them, the chances are good that they will be clear to your congregation.

Again, draw from contemporary life some experience that will throw light on theological ideas and language. Both can seem very abstract and remote from the life of your people. Suppose you are preaching about redemption. Paul took the term from slavery, and its underlying idea is liberation.

I remember meeting a boy when I was returning home from Europe after World War II. He had been released from a German prison camp only a few months before. The marks of the privation of that camp were still on his life. He told me about the day when they heard the rumbling of tanks and knew they were American tanks coming to set them free. He said uncontrollable joy swept through the camp. The men laughed and cried, sang and prayed. They were now liberated from the enemy. That story could help shed light on the theological doctrine of redemption.

Further, tell a story. Nothing has the power to clarify like a story. Imagine your preaching on the greeting Paul most often sent to those early churches: "Grace to you and peace from God our Father and the Lord Jesus Christ." Grace came first, but why? You could tell the story about Paul's first meeting the living and resurrected Lord. He was morally bankrupt and brought empty hands to Christ. But Christ forgave him anyway. It was all of grace; it was a gift. It was only after Paul received grace that his tormented and troubled soul found peace.

Finally, relate your truth, if possible, to some current happening that has been psychologically captivating. This makes for clarity because you address your people at a time of heightened awareness. Jesus did this kind of thing. In the thirteenth chapter of Luke, Jesus refers to two then current tragedies. These sad stories were on the lips of everybody. They were told and retold, discussed and agonized over in families in the marketplace. Then Jesus related his theme of repentance to these two tragedies known the nation over. Could his audience ever forget the truth Jesus was driving home?

Second, simplicity. This, of course, is closely related to clarity. Simplicity makes for clarity.

This is best achieved by using simple language. Here is a good rule: Never use a complex word when a simple one will suffice, and use the minimal number of words to achieve maximum meaning. Don't carry excess verbal baggage. It is a burden to the preacher and those who hear him. Of course, there will be exceptions. Every discipline has its own lingo and theology is no exception. Sometimes you will have to use a theological term that is multisyllabic and difficult, but it should be explained.

Simple language should be put together in simple sentences. A complex sentence should not be used if a simple one will do. Sentences should be short and pungent. Yet, this rule has its exceptions. A sweeping idea which is like a panoramic landscape demands a more complex form of expression.

We can learn much from the Bible here. Have you ever thought how few attempts are made to define God in the Bible? It is as if the Bible has a reticence here. God must be too great to be expressed in our little human definitions of him. But note how simple the language is when the attempt is made: God is spirit, God is light, and God is love. Each definition has three little one-syllable words. Imagine it! Of course, language cannot always be that simple. Sometimes difficult words must be used, but simplicity is the rule.

When Henry P. VanDusen was president of Union Theological Seminary in New York, he suggested to sixty-eight famous theologians that each try to state, in three or four sentences, the essence of the Christian faith. The definitions offered by these men abounded with words like "atonement" and "redemption." D. T. Niles on the other hand said: "God made you. God loves you. God gave his Son for you. When you die you will go to God. When you meet a man in the road that is what you should say."[5]

Archbishop William Temple was once referred to as "the most renowned primate of the Church of England since the English Revolution," and it was said of him that "his concepts were profound but his language was simple."[6]

It was said of Clovis Chappell, the great Methodist preacher, that "he preached with simplicity which touched all classes of people . . . He spoke on the practical where men lived and used langauge that could be understood."[7]

Third, vividness. We need to see truth. While a sermon is an oral discourse addressed to the ear and not the eye, people hear best and remember longest the ideas that have a visual quality. The preacher needs to paint pictures with words.

Thomas Guthrie, who was a famous Scottish preacher of the nineteenth century, was a master of words in the pulpit. One day while visiting the studio of an artist, he criticized an unfinished picture and offered suggestions as to how it could be improved. The painter was offended that an amateur would criticize his work, and spoke harshly to him: "Dr. Guthrie, remember you are a preacher and not a painter!" Guthrie responded very sharply, "Beg your pardon, my good friend—I am a painter; only I paint in words, while you use brush and colors."

Jesus is our best example. He was an artist at painting pictures with words. His speech was vivid and ideas leaped out with visual power when he spoke. Hear him as he talked about the kingdom of heaven.

"The kingdom of heaven is like a grain of mustard seed which a man took and sowed in the field; it is the smallest of all seeds, but when it has grown it is the greatest of all shrubs and becomes a tree, so that the birds of the air come and make nests in its branches" (Matt. 13:31-32).

Jesus didn't talk about the kingdom of heaven abstractly. He talked about it with verbal pictures. Was he less profound because he did? Of course not. But see the pictures that leap out at us. A farmer took a grain of mustard seed, which is the smallest of all seeds, and planted it. It was so small that you wouldn't expect much from it. But it sprouted and grew. It kept on growing, and became a tree shooting out strong branches. The birds built their nests in those branches and rested in them. We are almost bombarded with visual imagery.

How can we achieve vividness in our preaching? The most obvious answer is use vivid language that creates imagery, and use words that have form and motion.

Body language can help make ideas vivid. The way we use our eyes and hands is very important in achieving this quality.

We need to look at our congregation. That helps establish a

warm and intimate relationship with them. Yet, do not gore them with your eyes. They need relief from what might be staring. If you are faithful to your ideas you will give total relief. If you are talking about a lofty idea, look up; if about an expansive, sweeping idea look out, and at the same time you will achieve vividness for your thought.

Gestures are important. Gestures should be faithful to the preacher, that is, they should be natural and a projection of himself; and they should be faithful to the ideas, that is, they should be appropriate. Gestures can dramatize ideas, set them in motion, and make them vivid. I had a student who knew how to make effective gestures with his hands. The class said he could carve out ideas with his hands.

Fourth, force or energy. The sermon needs to be dynamic.

A sermon may have perfect form but be missing in vitality and power. It can be like a dud which has the form of a bomb, but has something missing in its delicate mechanism. It does not explode. Or a sermon can be like a dried-up riverbed. The form is there, but no water flows through its channels. No ships sail there anymore.

How do you achieve this force in your style? Use strong nouns and strong verbs. Strong nouns express the muscularity of ideas while strong verbs express their vigorous action. Bishop Gerald Kennedy thought it was important to find "words to make thoughts march." Use adjectives and adverbs sparingly.

Again, preach with conviction suffused with feeling. It is tragic to hear a preacher mechanically parroting mighty ideas with no conviction and feeling.

Time magazine in its issue of December 31, 1979, selected seven ministers whom it called the seven star preachers of Protestantism. *Time* used three criteria in selecting them: "Those chosen had to convey, along with solid content and skillful delivery, the sense of overwhelming conviction that is one of the golden keys to great preaching." I was impressed by the importance given to conviction. It is indeed one of the golden keys to great preaching.

Further, the sermon must be vitalized by the preacher's experience. The preacher must know the grace of Christ in forgiveness and reconciliation. The gospel is something that has happened to him. Since it is good news to him, he believes that it can be good news to everybody else.

Finally, preaching must be empowered by the Holy Spirit. The gifts of the Spirit are many, but the Spirit's chief gift is power. Preaching is such an exciting and dynamic act in the New Testament, and one idea is made clear: The Holy Spirit has breathed life and vitality into it.

Fifth, specificity. Be specific. We can be so general that nothing specific and concrete is addressed. We can be like a man shooting a sawed-off shotgun, scattering shot everywhere, but hitting nothing in particular. We should be more like a man shooting a .22 caliber rifle with a target clearly defined.

Charles R. Brown told about a young seminary student who wanted above all things to be guarded in utterance. So one Sunday morning, with his head on one side and the *vox humana* stop in his voice pulled out full length, he said to his people: "My beloved hearers, if I may call you so, you are under some measure of moral obligation to repent, so to speak; and in case you do not, I would venture to suggest that there is a remote possibility that you may be doomed, as it were, to a certain extent."[8]

How do you escape falling into the trap of vagueness? You address the gospel to specific kinds of persons, situations, attitudes, problems, and decisions in such a way that your people can identify with them. They will respond like this: "I feel the judgment of God in that"; "I experience the grace of God's forgiveness"; "I am that person"; "We have that situation in our community"; "That problem exists right here in our church."

Again, you break a general truth down into specific ideas. Take the truth of Christian love. You can treat it so generally that it means everything but nothing in particular. The truth has to be broken down into specific relationships: What it means to love a person who does not love you; what it means to love a person of another race; what it means to love the neighbor down the street; what it means to love your own child; what it means to love yourself?

Finally, the proper use of language can help us. We use specific rather than general words.

H. Grady Davis can help us.[9] He lists two columns of words, general and specific.

General	Specific
Flowers	Apple blossoms
Ignorant savages	Pygmies from the center of Africa (Fosdick)
A great poet	John Milton
A dirty animal	A pig
Extreme suffering	Blood, toil, tears, sweat (Churchill)

It is obvious that the specific words are much more forceful. They pack a wallop whereas the general words do not.

Sixth, freshness. I mean something close to novelty, but not sensationalism.

Speak in such a way that people will say to themselves: *I never thought of it that way; That certainly is a fresh approach to truth; That is a new way of presenting an old truth; That is an arresting way of presenting that idea.*

Here are several examples which illustrate what I mean by freshness.

I remember a sermon on the good Samaritan in which the preacher spoke of three philosophies: Robber's: What is yours is mine and I will take it; the Priest's and Levite's: What is mine is mine and I'll keep it; the good Samaritan's: What is mine is yours and I'll share it with you.

Or another sermon on the good samaritan with this simple outline: Wounder, the Wounded, and the Wound-healer.

I recall a sermon on "The Three Crosses": The Reviling Thief: dying in sin; The Repentant Robber: dying to sin; Jesus: dying for sin.

Here is a simple outline on the prodigal son: Sick of Home, Homesick, Back Home.

I cannot forget a sermon on this text: "For you know the grace of our Lord Jesus Christ, that though he was rich, yet for your sake he became poor, so that by his poverty you might become rich" (2 Cor. 8:9). The sermon contrasted the story of Jesus with many American legends about those who went from rags to riches. The outline was simple: He Was Rich, He Became Poor, that we might become rich; but it was the title, "From Riches to Rags," that made the sermon unforgettable.

I want to mention a final sermon which had as its basis an early Christian hymn, Philippians 2:6-11, in which Jesus is pictured as being on an equality with God. Then he made a Precipitous Descent into the world; he became a man, lower still a servant, and lower still he died the most shameful death of the ancient world, that of the cross. Then Jesus Christ made a Steep Ascent, as precipitous as his descent, and was highly exalted "above every name." Before him all creation will at last bow and every tongue make the earliest of all Christian confessions: Jesus Christ is Lord. The outline was so simple—up, down, up again—you could not forget it.

Seventh, beauty. A sermon should have beauty, if for no

other reason because of its poetic nature.

Simple, chaste, unadorned language can be beautiful. "The style of an address," wrote Charles R. Brown, "like the style of a dress may be severely chaste and simple and yet elegant in the best sense of that term."[10]

J. W. Jowett told of Henry Drummond's addressing waifs in Edinburgh. They were a company of poor, ragged, neglected youngsters. Jowett had this to say about Drummond: "He spoke to them with a simplicity and finished refinement which added the spell of beauty to the vigor of truth."[11]

A sermon should have order, balance, and symmetry that make for beauty. Yet, the order should not be forced. Neither should the balance be artificial nor the symmetry too perfect. These qualities should be created in faithfulness to the truth that is to be presented.

Give attention to content, but also to style. Strive consistently to achieve a fine quality of style, else your people may forget your best sermon because its style was poor and remember your worst one because your style was good.

5
Giving Luster to the Sermon

The use of illustrations is important, and the preacher who masters the art of using them will have developed an essential skill for effective preaching. The illustrations are what people normally remember best and longest about the sermon. If a preacher changes the title, and that is not necessary unless it is arresting, and the illustrations, he can preach a sermon over and over again at intervals of a year or so, and the people will not recognize it. But if the illustrations are kept, the sermon will be easily recognizable.

If illustrations are what people remember best, they are obviously important.

FUNCTION

One has to understand the function of an illustration in order to understand its importance. Its function is to present truth clearly, vividly, and concretely.

Someone has said that illustrations are windows for the sermon. They let in light so the truth can be seen clearly. Illustration comes from the Latin *illustratus* which means illuminated. It bears a close kinship to luster which comes from the French *lustrare* meaning to shine. As a matter of fact luster is built into illustration. Truths that may be lost in the darkness of abstraction can be clearly seen if properly illustrated. Illustrations give luster to the sermon.

The illustration makes a truth vivid. It gives a visual quality to the ideas. It is true that a sermon is a spoken discourse, and therefore addressed to the ear, not to the eye. Yet, people hear best those ideas that are clothed in visual imagery. No matter how thoroughly a pastor has prepared a sermon, he should go over it carefully to see if his ideas have become visual. If they have not, he should rewrite the sermon.

The illustration also helps make the idea concrete. That is important since a truth presented concretely appeals to something very basic in our nature. We are not disembodied spirits. We have bodies. As already suggested, we can't be everywhere at once. We can be at only one place. For the most part we deal with particulars, not generalities; with specifics, not abstractions. We live in a certain town, on a particular street, with a specific house number. We don't do everything. Rather, we follow a specific vocation or trade. We know individual people with given names, bodily features, and personality traits, not abstract humanity. We see a human being, not the face of the human race. Because the face is not an abstraction, we either love or hate it. We give anthropomorphic features to God. We speak of his face, his voice, or his footsteps. This we do, not because we believe God is a man, but because metaphors make truth concrete.

I have labored this, because concreteness is a part of our basic nature. When truth, therefore, is presented concretely, it appeals to something deep and primordial in us. It is little wonder that an illustration is an effective tool of communication.

If you would see a master of illustration, study Jesus. He was highly skilled in the use of simile, metaphor, and story as vehicles of truth.

Take for example Jesus' story of the prodigal son. Truth is made clear. We understand how reckless and irresponsible freedom leads to bondage; what it is to be lost from where you should be, and from those to whom you really belong; how God, like the father, accepts us unconditionally in his great love; and how legalism, as seen in the elder brother, dries up the springs of human compassion, leaving one loveless, harsh, and self-righteous. Truth is made vivid. A visual quality is given to Jesus' great insights. We see repentance in the younger brother as he turns home, compassion in the father as he embraces the way-ward boy, and we see loneliness and separation in the elder brother who stands in the shadows of the banquet hall, refusing to go in. And truth is made concrete. There is a pigsty with a young man so hungry that he is tempted to eat what the pigs leave; there is a father weeping on the shoulder of his returning son; there are sandals, a ring, a robe, and a fatted calf; and there is a banquet table with happy people gathered around it, making merry.

A GOOD ILLUSTRATION

What makes a good illustration?

First, obviously a good illustration fulfills its basic functions; that of making truth clear, vivid, and concrete. An illustration that makes truth dull, obscure, or abstract aborts its purpose.

I remember a student using an illustration in a sermon that was opaque and obscure. Rather than throwing light on the sermon, the sermon had to throw light on it. Rather than explaining the sermon, the sermon had to explain the illustration. That was a bad illustration.

Further, a good illustration must throw into focus some important truth. It must deal with some great theme of life such as love, sacrifice, courage, forgiveness, reconciliation, or broken relationships healed. It does not deal with trivial and unimportant matters.

Take for example an illustration on courage and sacrifice as represented by Samuel Pisor, an international lawyer who is a survivor of the terrible holocaust in Europe. He was thirteen when he was taken from home and put into a concentration camp. He was the only survivor of his family. The experience was so painful that he still finds it difficult to talk about.

He remembers the last day he saw his mother. She knew she was condemned, but she wanted her son to survive. As a part of achieving this, she stifled deep feelings in her life. She talked about the clothes he would wear almost as casually as if she were selecting them for him to go to a summer camp. Would he wear long or short pants? She chose long pants. They might make him appear more as a man and be spared for the labor force. Then, rather than taking him in her arms, which was an almost irrestible impulse, she did what seemed to be heartless: she shoved him away from her. It was as if she pushed him to independence. Of that Pisor said: "My mother gave me a second life that day, more painful to her than the first she gave me." What a story of courage and sacrifice!

Finally, a good illustration has both simplicity and depth. If complex, it cannot shed light. It should not be too polished and ornamental. That removes it too far from life. It should have something of the rough-hewn nature of life about it. An illustration that comes from where people sweat and work with their hands is normally better than one from the opulent and leisured styles of the few. And a good illustration has depth. Sophistication, as well as pomp and ceremony, is on the surface. It is veneer. Let the illustration come from those depths where people laugh and weep, hope and despair, believe and doubt, where life bleeds but can be healed.

Bishop Gerald Kennedy gave many an illustration that had both simplicity and depth. I think of one in particular. As he was getting his hair cut, his barber was talking about the astronauts going around the moon. "Wasn't that great?" he asked. "It sure was," Kennedy replied. "And wasn't that wonderful," his barber continued, "when they read from the Book of Genesis as they circled the moon? You know, Bishop, that was the only book big enough for men doing what they were doing and being where they were to read from." Bishop Kennedy made this comment about the experience: "What a fine insight it was! So much of the modern attempts to heal our worries are like rubbing a little salve on the cancer. It is only Christian faith that is big enough to bring the healing for men caught up in the troubles of human existence."[1]

SOURCES OF ILLUSTRATIONS

How do you go about finding illustrations? What are their sources?

The best source is from your own experience with the contemporary world. You are most effective when you are speaking about those things you have seen, heard, handled, and experienced.

Jesus drew his stories and illustrations from the world he and his hearers knew. He talked about rocky and rich soil, mustard seeds, wheat, the rainy seasons when wadis overflowed their shallow channels, sheep, and goats. This was the nature they knew. He talked about masters, slaves, soldiers, farmers, shepherds, merchants, builders, priests, and Levites. These were the people they knew. He talked about losing things and the joy of finding them, laughter and tears, faith and doubt, work and play, prayer and worship. These were experiences they knew.

Paul also did this. He went to the great cities, established churches there, and wrote his letters to those churches. He talked about the Greek races, Roman soldiers, courts, guardians, masters, slaves, and the family structure he knew. He drew metaphors from his world by which to describe the church: the church as a body, temple, garden, commonwealth, and family. His hearers understood these.

We should do the same thing. We should be open to our world with its labor and leisure, its health and suffering, its joy and sorrow. Somebody has said that we should look out upon our world through the eyes of "mature childhood." To see it through the eyes of childhood is to see surprise, wonder, mystery in life. But to see it through the eyes of maturity is to see it realistically.

There is a need of caution: We should not see our world through sermonic eyes. We do not look out on our world just to find sermon ideas and illustrations. I heard George Buttrick comment that there is nothing more hideous than the sermonic eye. I didn't know what he meant until one year I traveled with a fellow minister to a summer conference. He kept saying: "I see a sermon in that" or "There is a sermon illustration." I was bored. He cheapened both his world and his preaching. Rather, we should be open, eager, and sensitive to our world, enjoying it for itself, and not using it for sermonic ends. When we are, we will find plenty of sermon suggestions and illustrations without looking for them.

What we see may be either religious or secular. Since preaching is a religious act, we may be more comfortable with religious illustrations than secular ones, but this should not be so. Most of Jesus' stories were secular to the core. Since God is not only Lord of the temple and altar but all of life, the secular can be a vehicle of his truth and grace.

Somebody asked Ernest Campbell how he went about getting ideas and illustrations for his sermons. He pulled from his pocket a small notebook and held it before the group. Whenever he had an experience that gripped him, whether from nature, people, reading a book, or a flash of insight, he jotted it down in his little notebook. He had filled up several of these. They all came from his world and his experience.

What about illustrations drawn from a technological culture? Frankly, illustrations drawn from the technical side of life are usually not good. Stories about tanks, planes, rockets, and satellites are poor unless the human element is stressed and thrown into focus. The reason for this is that they tell of an I-it relationship. Great illustrations come out of an I-thou relationship. The best illustrations are about relationships—broken and healed.

Again, biography is a good source of illustrations.

The Bible puts more stress on the corporate life than we do. We are more conscious of the personal and individual life. Yet, the corporate life of the Bible is more than the faceless mass. Individuals, strong and purposeful, emerge. When the author of Hebrews reflects on the meaning of their history, he thinks not so much of the nation's faith as the faith of national heroes. These great men and women, who caught a vision of God and followed it without faltering, bestrode their history like giants.

The stories of brave men and women, who love God and their fellows and who are faithful during unfaithful times are vehicles of grace and truth. These men and women may come from the past, even the remote past, but they still have a powerful word. They, being dead, yet speak. But these stories are probably more effective when they are about people from our time and world. They are our contemporaries and we are more aware of them.

Take, for example, Mother Teresa of Calcutta who is our contemporary. She is one of the great Christians of our generation. A prominent minister said if he were given the privilege of spending an hour with any person of our world, he would spent it with Mother Teresa. She has given her life to the feeding of the poor and starving of India. She was the winner of the Nobel Peace Prize for 1979. She declined the dinner planned in her honor, asking that the money be given to feed the hungry people in India. In her acceptance speech she talked about the peace and dignity with which the poor die. Then she told about a man whom they had taken from the streets into their home so he could die with dignity. He was emaciated and his body was covered with maggots. In response to their kindess, he said: "I have lived like an animal in the streets. Here I shall die like an angel." Mother Teresa said that in his last hours he was somebody to somebody. What a powerful story to illustrate Christian compassion.

Further, history is another source of illustrations. Christian truth is at home in history since God reveals himself through history. God saves us, not out of history, but in it. The gospel we preach is therefore no stranger to history and often history affords us good vehicles for the truth we preach. Someone, reflecting on God's action in history, said history is his story.

If you are preaching on courage born of prayer, you might tell about George Washington and his troops during the winter at Valley Forge. His troops were poorly fed, poorly clothed, and poorly sheltered. They suffered during that severe winter and their morale was low. They could see their moods reflected in the low, dark clouds of the winter sky. The situation often seemed desperate and hopeless. Washington, more than anyone else, bolstered the flagging morale of the troops. One day he was seen kneeling in the snow praying. Prayer, without doubt, was a source, maybe his greatest source, of courage. He could feel that God was on the side of freedom and justice.

Or we might turn to the contemporary historical situation to stress the interdependence of life and nations. We are beginning to see that, not only are small nations dependent on big ones, but powerful nations are also dependent on the small ones. Witness how dependent for oil powerful industrial nations are on weaker ones like Iran and Saudi Arabia. We understand better than we once did how important the backward and undeveloped countries are in the family of nations. History is like a vast ocean liner and we are all on board. If it sinks, we will all go down; if it makes port, we will all arrive. We are slow to learn that lesson, and if we learn it at all, it will be painful. But learn it we must if we are to survive.

Again music, especially hymns, is an excellent source for illustrations. Hymns have had more influence on our lives than most of us know. They likely have had almost as great influence on our theology and the shaping of our spiritual lives as the Bible. Stories about the great and familiar hymns are often very effective.

If you are preaching on spiritual security, you might tell with good effect a story about Charles Wesley's inspiration to write his great hymn, "Jesus, Lover of My Soul." Wesley stood before an open window watching an approaching storm. Driven by the strong winds of the storm a little bird flew through the window into Wesley's bosom. There the bird was safe. This experience inspired Wesley to write:

> Jesus, lover of my soul,
> Let me to thy bosom fly,
> While the nearer waters roll,
> While the tempest still is high.

Also, literature may be a source of illustrations. Poets, novelists, and dramatists may be more in touch with the anguish of life than theologians, may ask more poignantly the profound questions about life, and may speak of spiritual truth in fresher frameworks.

Suppose you are preaching on the emptiness and vacuity of modern life. T. S. Eliot's poem, "The Hollow Men," might help illustrate your truth:

We are the hollow men
We are the stuffed men
Leaning together
Headpiece filled with straw. Alas!

Again, let me mention art as a source of illustrations. Classic paintings and sculptures, like great music and literature, can tremendously aid in articulating and illustrating truth.

In preaching on love and faith in the face of tragedy, you could describe Michelangelo's *Pietá* with moving effect. The youthful-looking Mary is holding her dead son in her lap. It seems to be pure tragedy. Jesus had done nothing to deserve death. If Jesus had been killed by gangsters and hoodlums, his death would not have been quite so puzzling. But he had not met his death that way. The most respectable forces of his day had put him to death. Organized religion, the keeper of faith and morality, and the state, the guardian of law and order, had joined hands to put him to death. You see in the face of Mary anguish and pain, but the light of faith and love shines there. And peace and serenity are also in her face. What sustained her? A faith in a loving providence that at last overrides all tragedy. The resurrection would confirm her faith in ways she could not know.

Finally, the Bible is an excellent source of illustrations. Scripture is the best interpreter of Scripture. The Bible has wonderful stories that amplify its truths.

Suppose you are preaching on liberation which is one of the overarching themes of the Bible. You could find no better illustrations than those in the Book. You might tell the story of the Exodus where helpless slaves were delivered into freedom by the mighty hand of God. It was such a dramatic experience and is the towering event of the Old Testament. Or you could tell the story about the death of Jesus who was crucified on a Roman cross, which was in that time what the electric chair is in our own, except it was even more shameful. But it is by the death of Jesus that men and women are set free from the enslavement of sin. Or take the resurrection of Jesus. Jesus fought death where death is king—in a tomb, and he won. His empty tomb was left against a dawn. There is where we are set free from the imprisonment of our death.

MISTAKES TO BE AVOIDED

Like anything with promising possibilities, illustrations can be badly misused and mishandled. There are certain mistakes to be avoided. Let me mention five of these.

First, don't choose an illustration and build a sermon around it. The illustration is not to be lord; it is to be servant. It is to serve the sermon rather than the sermon's serving it. It is to amplify the sermon, rather than the sermon's amplifying it.

I remember a young man preaching in a workshop. He loved to preach. He was enthusiastic and gifted. He had a wonderful illustration. It soon became apparent what he had done. He felt almost compulsively that he must use that illustration which had captivated his imagination. The illustration came first—then the sermon. The sermon served the purpose of the illustration, rather than the illustration serving the sermon. While the illustration was most meaningful, the sermon suffered because of it.

Again, don't allow illustrations to be too long. When they are, they have an undue prominence. As already said, they are to be servants, not lords.

We often make the mistake of believing an illustration has to be a story of length, whereas it may be a simile or a metaphor. It can be very short. Jesus was a master in using the simile and metaphor. You remember how he said the kingdom of heaven is like a mustard seed, like leaven which a woman took and hid in three measures of flour, like a treasure buried in a field, like a merchant in search of fine pearls, or like a net that was thrown into the sea. These are similes but they clarify, make vivid, and concretize the truth. They throw light on the truth. Or see how skillfully Jesus used metaphors: I am the light of the world, the bread of life, the door, the way, the truth, and the life. They are brief but also apt illustrations. They are like a shaft of light falling on the truth which might be shadowed and dark without them.

Harry Emerson Fordick was a master of illustrations. Yet, most of his illustrations were short. His sermons averaged twelve or fifteen illustrations, but often they were little more than a vivid image.

Further, don't string illustrations together with little substance for them to amplify. When you do that, it is like having a building whose sides are windows and whose rooms are poorly furnished. The light comes streaming in, falling on emptiness.

Also, illustrations are not to be complex and opaque. They are to throw light on truth of greater complexity. When the sermon has to explain the illustration, rather than the illustration explaining the sermon, something is wrong. Keep illustrations simple. This is a rule that allows for no exceptions.

Finally, don't use illustrations that are stale. You might choose an illustration that is appropriate to the idea and yet is like musty air. It is not fresh. It is not alive.

I remember a student who had a flair for using illustrations. He knew how to match the illustration and truth. Sometimes, though, the illustration seemed to fit too neatly the idea, and his illustrations were missing in freshness, vitality, and immediacy. I asked him where he found them, and he confessed—from a book of illustrations. I had suspected as much.

You should be very careful and discriminating in selecting illustrations. It is not enough that they have tickled your fancy and imagination. They should have gripped your life profoundly and significantly. If they have, they will not grow stale but will remain fresh and lively. A simple way to keep them is to write them topically in a loose-leaf notebook.

We hear a lot of criticism about preaching being dry and boring. It often seems abstract, far beyond the hearers, or remote from their lives. There is nothing better to correct this than to become a master of the illustration. Work hard at it.

6
Preaching as Narrative

We hear much about gospel as story, preaching as narrative, and preacher as storyteller. We will be hearing more about preaching as narrative. This method is gathering momentum. It has always been an effective and legitimate preaching form, but we have become more aware of it in our time.

The communication environment is changing. We have been accustomed to straight talk and honest and rugged confrontation. We have pulled no punches, left nothing unsaid that we thought should be said. Now this is changing. "I think story preaching has become possible in our culture today precisely because the communication environment we have been describing has changed," writes Richard A. Jensen. "People have grown weary of constant eyeball to eyeball confrontation and direct encounters. The signs that this is the case, the signs that the communication environment in which we live has altered, are increasingly visible. Stories have a future among us."[1]

We have prized science and technology, and have been greatly influenced by them. But they have robbed us of something priceless. They have left our imaginations unmoved and our hearts unfilled. They have dissected and analyzed life while we long for wholeness. We want our imaginations moved, our hearts stirred, and life held in fullness again. Nothing can do that better than the story. Is it any wonder that we are hungry for it again?

Story has always been one of the best, if not the best, form of human communication. Tell a story well and the child and most sophisticated person in your congregation will listen. When you begin "once upon a time" everyone pricks up their ears. You get an audience immediately. But why? Story is in touch with reality in a manner other forms of communication are not. Life is story, and only story knows that secret.

GOSPEL AS STORY

Our whole Bible is concerned with gospel, with good news. From beginning to end the Bible tells how God loves and affirms his world, cannot give it up, performs saving deeds, and takes extreme action in order that it may be brought back to himself. All of this saving and redemptive action reaches its climax in Jesus Christ. The Christ event is God's ultimate effort to save us.

The Bible uses many literary forms to tell of God's redemptive plan. It uses law, history, poetry, drama, wisdom, prophecy, gospel, letters, apocalypse, and story. But there is a sense in which all the other literary forms of the Bible are beads strung on the string of story. There is a running, sequential action in the Bible that only story can tell.

I have already stated that life is story. Add to that another wonderful reality: Our faith is story.

Robert McAfee Brown, thinking in terms of our faith as story, has written: "We must recover the story if we are to recover a faith for our day. Each of us has his or her story. Alongside them is the Christian story, a story of the heroes and heroines of the faith. Could the pair of stories impact one another? Sometimes we hear another person's story and we say, 'aha! that's my story too.' In hearing about Abraham Lincoln or Jane Addams . . . or Coretta King, I am learning about myself!

Our theological task is to find ways 'to tell the old, old story' so that the listener can say 'aha! that's my story too.' In hearing about Abraham or Sarah or Jeremiah or Judas I am learning about myself."[2]

Think about the biblical truths we learned first and earliest, and incidentally remembered best. What are they? They are truths told in stories.

What are some of these stories we learned first and remember best? The story of Adam and Eve in a beautiful garden they were to keep and the tempting fruit they were not to eat. There was in that garden a serpent, the symbol of evil, slithering in the dust, who tempted them to eat of the forbidden fruit and they yielded. Now guilty, Adam and Eve hid from God, and God, walking in the garden in the cool of the day, called them. Their sin became known to God and his terrible judgment came down on them. They were cast out of the garden to become homeless, wandering vagabonds on the face of the earth. We learned that story before we did its theology, but the theology was in the story from the beginning.

Then there is the story of the Flood which was God's devastating judgment on the people of the earth whose "imagination of the thoughts of [the] heart was only evil continually" (Gen. 6:5). Only Noah's family was saved. Noah gathered animals of every species into an ark which rode out the turbulent waters of the flood. So history began over again. And God set a gorgeous ranbow in the sky as a promise that he would never again destroy the earth with a flood.

We learned about ambitious men with overweening pride starting to build the Tower of Babel designed to reach into the heavens. They would usurp God's power and become gods, and God came down, scattered them, and divided them with the high barriers of language.

We have not forgotten the story of Joseph who was sold into slavery by his jealous brothers and who by a remarkable turn of events became prime minister of Egypt. In later years there was the poignant but joyful meeting of Joseph with his brothers who, having been driven by famine, had come to Egypt to buy grain.

We think of the greatest of all the Old Testament stories, that of the Exodus. The groans of the oppressed Israelites, who were slaves in Egypt, went up to God who heard them. Then came the sending of Moses to Pharaoh, king of Egypt, the terrible plagues visited on Pharaoh and the Egyptians, and the dramatic deliverance at the Red Sea. This is a wonderful story that carries in it the exciting theology of liberation.

There are many, many more stories we have known since childhood. Think of the stories about Abraham, Isaac, Jacob, Elijah, Amos, Hosea, Isaiah, Jeremiah, Daniel, and others.

When we come to the New Testament, it is the stories we recall best. From childhood we have remembered the Christmas stories. Among our most treasured imagery are the star in the East, shepherds and Wise Men, Joseph and Mary, and the baby in swaddling clothes lying in a manger. What we recall best about Jesus is not his formal teachings, as important as they are, but stories about him. Especially do we think of two stories about Jesus, those of his death and resurrection which have always been at the center of the Christian gospel.

In Acts we do not have a theory and logistic of missions discussed. We have stories about Paul and others taking the gospel to the cities of that world, the responsiveness and resistance with which they met, and their leaving behind them churches as they moved on.

The letters of Paul and others are not stories as such, yet stories often appear in them. As for example, the lovely story about the runaway slave, Onesimus, being returned to Philemon, his master, to whom Paul commends the returning slave as a beloved brother.

Why do we remember the stories of our faith better than

other forms through which it is communicated? Obviously, because our faith is best told by a story.

Henry H. Mitchell, writing of black preaching, has said: "The black pulpit is at its best when the gospel is communicated in the form of a folk story. That is to say, there is no better vehicle for the unforgettable portrayal of a powerful truth than an engaging tale."[3]

PREACHING AS NARRATIVE

Edmund Steimle, distinguished preacher and teacher of homiletics believes the story is the most basic and effective form of preaching. The sermon "takes the form of a story told," he writes, "as a whole or in its parts. It is not strange that this is so because, to come back to Wilder again, 'all life has the character of a story and a plot' . . . Each sermon should have something of the dramatic form of a play or short story: tightly knit, one part leading into and dependent upon the next, with some possibility of suspense and surprise evident in the development and the end."[4]

There is much evidence that supports Steimle's opinion, and nothing is more convincing than the fact that Jesus used the story in preaching and teaching. The story was his basic form of communication. Jesus was an artist who used words to paint pictures, and as we read his stories, ideas leap out at us with visual power.

Jesus did not think abstractly but concretely, and his method of communication was appropriate to his kind of thinking. In response to a lawyer's question, "Who is my neighbor?" (Luke 10:29) Jesus did not answer theoretically. He told a story about the good Samaritan. The world would soon have forgotten a philosophical discussion of the subject, but the world has never forgotten the story he told. Indeed we can never forget it. We are still telling it, and no story has ever stirred so much social compassion.

When Jesus wanted to contrast the life of legalism with the life of grace, he told a story about two men, a Pharisee and a tax collector, who went up into the Temple to pray. The Pharisee prayed arrogantly, "God, I thank thee that I am not like other men," but the tax collector standing far away in the shadows prayed, "God, be merciful to me a sinner" (Luke 18:10,13). The tax collector threw himself heavily on the grace of God, and God heard his prayers, while turning a deaf ear to the Pharisee.

Jesus, knowing how deceptive and treacherous wealth is with its lure of power, told about a rich farmer. He had been very successful, tearing down his old barns to build larger and better ones, and had said to himself: "Soul, you have ample goods laid up for many years; take your ease, eat, drink, be merry." When he was at the height of his power, God, like a voice crying out at the midnight hour, said to him: "Fool! This night your soul is required of you; and the things you have prepared, whose will they be?" (Luke 12:19-20).

When Jesus wanted to talk about social justice he didn't give a new code of laws. He told a story. With bold verbal strokes, Jesus pictured a man without social compassion who "was clothed in purple and fine linen and who feasted sumptuously every day" (Luke 16:19). At the gate of this socially insensitive man lay Lazarus, a beggar, full of sores which scavenger dogs licked. The poor man hoped to be given the leftovers from the rich man's table. Then both of them died, and the situation was radically changed: Lazarus is in heaven and the rich man is in hell. We are still telling that story and as we do we should remember that its purpose is not merely to describe hell. It is also about social justice.

When Jesus wanted to talk about the grace of God that accepts us fully and unconditionally, he didn't give a theological discourse. Once again he told a story. God is like a father who accepted back into the family a profligate boy who had returned friendless, penniless, and in rags. The father didn't reject him, didn't even put him on probation, but accepted him fully. God is like that. He accepts us exactly as we are, rags and all.

In further support of preaching as story, early Christian preaching made effective use of the narrative form, as is obvious from the study of sermons in Acts.

Peter's Pentecostal sermon begins with a burning concern for his congregation which is a good place to begin. Get their attention. There is no use to preach if your congregation is not listening. The people thought those Christians, now filled with the Holy Spirit, were drunk with wine at 9 o'clock in the morning. That was very unusual, to say the least. Peter assured them that this was not the case. This strange behavior was the fulfilling of a prophecy by Joel who had promised that God would pour out his Spirit upon all flesh in the last days. It was such a tremendous moment. They were standing on the threshold of the new age, as the lengthening shadows of the old age were passing into night. Then Peter turned quickly to narrative when he told them briefly the story of Jesus of Nazareth, attested by God, yet crucified. But the grave could not keep him. He was resurrected, then took his place at the right hand of God, from where he had poured out the Holy Spirit upon the believers in Jesus. God had taken this Crucified One and made him both Lord and Christ. The response to Peter's sermon was overwhelming.

Recorded in the seventh chapter of Acts is the heart of Stephen's sermon which he preached in the synagogue of the Freedmen. It was a powerful sermon and it was narrative. He began with God's calling Abraham while he still lived in Mesopotamia. Then he briefly traced Israel's history through Abraham and the patriarchs. He gave considerable attention to Joseph's being sold into Egypt, later followed there by his family, the enslavement in Egypt, the call of Moses, the deliverance at the Red Sea, the giving of the law at Mount Sinai, the disobedience of the people, and their return to idolatry, and their being settled in the Promised Land under Joshua.

Then Stephen picked up the story with David and Solomon. As the people had been stiff-necked and rebellious in the wilderness, so they had always been, and so they were still. Their fathers persecuted and killed the prophets who announced the coming of the Righteous One. And now that the Righteous One, Jesus of Nazareth, had come, they had betrayed and murdered him. With this, bedlam broke out and Stephen was not able to continue his story through the resurrection of Jesus, his ascension to the right hand of God, and his gift of the Holy Spirit. If Stephen had talked abstractly about Israel's faith and history, he might not have gotten into trouble, but the narrative was pungently powerful!

Paul's sermon at Antioch of Pisidia, which is recorded in the thirteenth chapter of Acts, is one of the best preserved from the preaching of the early church, and once more it is narrative. Paul began with the bondage in Egypt and the deliverance of the Israelites from slavery. By so doing he entered straight into the heart of Israel's faith which centered in the Exodus. Israel was concerned with the great themes of bondage and freedom just as Christians are. Then Paul moved the story through the wandering in the wilderness, the conquest and settlement of Canaan, the rule of the judges, and finally the anointing of Saul as Israel's first king. Next, Paul told of David from whose posterity "God has brought to Israel, a Savior, Jesus, as he promised" (v. 23). John the Baptist, the forerunner of Jesus, who preached a "baptism of repentance to all the people of Israel" (v. 24) was mentioned. Finally he recounted the trial, death, and resurrection of Jesus. Against this background, Paul preached the heart of the Christian gospel: "Let it be known to you therefore, brethren, that through this man forgiveness of sins is proclaimed to you, and by him every one that believes is freed from everything from which you could not be freed by the law of Moses" (vv. 38-39).

It was a very powerful sermon. As they left, the people begged them to return the next sabbath. On that day "almost the whole city gathered together to hear the word of God" (Acts 13:44). Philosophical and abstract ideas could not have moved the people that way, but the narrative did.

The modern world is very different from the world in which the gospel was first preached. Yet, we should not forget that the gospel we have is not a new one but the same one Paul, Peter, and others of the early church proclaimed. While our culture is much different from that of the first century, human nature and the basic human problems are what they have always been, and we should remember that a narrative well told is as effective and moving today as it was when Jesus was telling his incomparably beautiful stories.

I have a friend who, speaking of my last Sunday's sermon, will always ask: "Did you tell the story?" It is indeed a good question, probably better than he knows. Many a sermon that is abstract, difficult, and boring, failing to stimulate the imagination and move the heart, could be completely transformed if preached in narrative form.

THE PREACHER AS STORYTELLER

Storytelling is an art, and like all arts it has to be cultivated. Since it is such a basic preaching form, we should work at storytelling.

Let me suggest that we do three things with narrative in the pulpit: Tell stories, retell stories with a modern setting, and give a narrative quality to sermons that are not stories as such.

First, tell stories. These stories may be biblical, secular, or personal.

The story you tell may be biblical such as the Tower of Babel, the call of Abraham, Joseph in Egypt, Isaiah's transforming experience in the Temple, Paul's conversion, or one of the parables of Jesus. All of these stories have a theological significance that is just as pertinent as when they occurred or were first told.

The story may be secular. Don't be afraid to tell a secular story. Jesus wasn't. Despite the wonderful stories he knew from the Old Testament, his stories were secular, being lifted from the life of his time. That is one of the most interesting things about his approach. We can't help asking: Why were his stories secular? We would not like to give a dogmatic answer, but likely because he knew his hearers for the most part lived their lives in a secular world. These stories touched their lives. These were the stories they understood best. Jesus told these stories in the firm faith that God worked in the secular as well as the sacred, that he could be present at the carpenter's bench as well as at the altar.

I remember several years ago when I realized that so many of God's saving acts as recorded in the Bible, occurred in the secular world, not at altars presided over by priests. It was indeed a shocking revelation. The Exodus, which is the Old Testament's towering event, occurred not in a temple but at the Red Sea. There could scarcely have been found a more secular place in the ancient world. Barges of commerce sailed on its waters and caravan routes skirted its shores. There were on that day of deliverance, of course, screams of people fleeing for freedom which were like prayers lifted to God, but there was the grinding of chariot wheels, the neighing of horses, the cursing of cavalry officers, and the profanity of soldiers. Jesus was not born in the precinct of a temple but in a manger, was more layman than priest, was crucified, not on an altar but on a barren hill outside the city wall, was not buried in a sacred crypt but in a borrowed tomb, and ascended not from the pinnacle of the Temple but from the Mount of Olives. Yet, this is not to say that God does not reveal himself in the sacred. He does. Moses received the Ten Commandments from Mt. Sinai, which was likely a sacred mountain; Isaiah experienced his commissioning to be a prophet in the Temple; and Jesus gave his inaugural address in his home synagogue.

Yet, secular stories should be used with discrimination. We should ask at least two questions about them: Do they shed light on the human situation, and can they be vehicles of the gospel?

I served as graves registration officer for my battalion for several months in Sicily during World War II. It was my duty with a contingency of soldiers to find our men who had been killed and move their bodies to collection points along the highway. One day we came across a German soldier who two days earlier had suffered a serious lower abdominal wound and during that time had been dragging himself over the hills under a hot Sicilian sun. Because of the heat and loss of blood he was dying from thirst. I shall never forget how he screamed "vater! vater!" when he saw our canteen cups. We gave him water, and he lived.

This is a purely secular story but it can be used with good effect in a sermon. It certainly sheds light on the human situation and it can be a vehicle of the gospel. It can speak for Christ who invites thirsty people everywhere to come to him and drink of the water of life.

Then there is the personal story which should be told sparingly, but there are times when it can be used with good effect. There are times when it should be used.

There are many things people want to see in us who stand in the pulpit, but one of the things they want most to believe is that the gospel we preach has become good news for us. They want to feel that gospel is something that has happened to us. A personal story, properly told with the right motive, can be very effective in communicating this.

Paul spoke often of his conversion when he met the living Lord along the Damascus road. He told it to commoners and kings. He never apologized for telling it. He wanted to tell it. He felt he should tell it.

I remember city-wide evangelistic campaigns years ago when we brought well-known evangelists to our community. Always there would be the night when the evangelist told his personal story. That was the night I did not want to miss. There is nothing more moving than for a person to tell how Christ in wonderful grace changed his life.

I have cautioned against using the personal story too frequently. One more word of caution: In telling a personal story don't put yourself beneath your people which demeans you, nor above them which demeans them. If you were born in a shanty in a cotton field somewhere, don't tell that over and over again. That demeans you. On the other hand if you were born with a silver spoon in your mouth, don't tell that either. It would demean some of your people. Both are bad. Let your story put you alongside them in their struggle, pain, and hope, and let your experience be one with which they can identify.

Second, retell a parable of Jesus or some other story from the Bible, putting it in a modern setting.

Wellford Hobbie tells about serving as a young pastor in tobacco country. During the barning season, a farmer might go out several times during the day for workers. He told the parable of the workers in the vineyard in the setting of the tobacco country. At the end of the day, the farmer paid all of them the same wages. The people who began the day's work at seven in the morning and those who came at noon, and at three o'clock in the afternoon received the same pay. There was the surprise that all experienced, and there was the hostility and resentment of those who had worked all day long. This parable, of course, points to the dimension of grace where the important thing is not how much we earn but the gift of that which we could never earn.

Third, even when the form of the sermon is not story, a narrative quality should be introduced to clarify abstract ideas.

All of your sermons will not be stories. Indeed, most of

them likely will not be. There is a place for abstract and conceptual thinking as earlier indicated. But abstract thinking needs to be clarified. One of the best ways of achieving this is by bringing a narrative quality to bear on it.

Henry H. Mitchell has written concerning this: "Nothing important should be said by syllogism which is not also stated more comprehensively in symbolic story, poetry, or picture."[5]

When preaching on justification by faith, which is one of the most difficult concepts in the New Testament, it should be remembered that justification was a term Paul borrowed from the courts. It would be effective to tell a story about Paul visiting a Roman court, which he might frequently have done as a boy. Imagine a day when he was caught up in the excitement of the trial. He could not keep his eyes off the man who had been arraigned. Was he guilty? Paul listened to the prosecutor and defense attorney as they strongly argued the case. Then came the dramatic moment when the judge would announce his decision. What would it be? Then the judge broke the suspense. "I declare this man just before this court," he said. Paul felt that was what God had said, except in a much more wonderful way, the day he trusted Jesus as the Messiah: "I declare you a just man before me." God pronounced Paul just for no other reason than that he had exercised faith in Jesus Christ. It was indeed justification by faith.

Whether you tell a story, retell a story, or give a narrative quality to a sermon which tends to be abstract, two things are indispensable if you are to be effective. First, your life has to intersect the story you tell. It has to become your story. Second, your congregation has to be able to identify with the story. It has to become their story, too. When these two indispensables are met, preaching as narrative can be powerful indeed.

I remember a student who used a narrative sermon with real effectiveness. He told about two mood swings in one day.

He began the day hopefully, feeling good about his church and its ministry. Then he heard nothing but criticism as he visited that day. "What's wrong with us?" asked one person. "People don't come. They start but stop," remarked another person. And from still another: "This is a one-family church." The day that began in hope ended in depression. Then he told the story about Elijah fleeing the wrathful Jezebel, and finally despairing of life. He was so depressed that he wanted to die. He felt that he alone was left to defend Yahweh. As this young man preached, you knew that Elijah's story had become his own.

The students who heard their fellow student preach found themselves identifying with his experience. They were saying in effect: "I know what he is talking about. I have been there. That very thing has happened to me." His story had become theirs. It was a very moving experience.

Let it be said that there is a wonderful thing about the stories of the Bible. They came out of life, and because they did you can identify with them. You are often able to say: "That's my story, too."

If Jesus told stories, and if early preaching, powerful as it was, made use of narrative, we should give serious attention to our being storytellers and our preaching using the narrative. If we will, many a sermon, which otherwise might be abstract, dull, and uninteresting, can be very vital and effective.

7
Empowered by the Holy Spirit

I still remember the day I realized that the Holy Spirit, next to Jesus Christ, is in some basic sense the greatest reality in the New Testament. That was an exciting discovery. Since that day, my theology and my preaching have not been the same.

Preaching is a challenging and difficult task. Anyone who doesn't realize that has not come to grips with the realities of the modern pulpit. The truth is we need all the help we can get, and one of our greatest sources of help is the Holy Spirit. The Holy Spirit makes power available to us and preaching cannot be really dynamic unless it is empowered by the Holy Spirit.

THE REALITY OF THE HOLY SPIRIT

The Holy Spirit, or Spirit of God, is God present in his world. When God created his world, he did not abandon it. He was not like a boy, setting his top spinning only to go off and leave it, letting it lose momentum and eventually run down. It is true that God stands above his creation like a craftsman who stands above the work of his hands. The fartherest star, wherever it is, is beyond the power of our mightiest telescope to find, but God is above that star. He transcends all things he has made. But God can be inside his creation in a way a craftsman can never be in the thing he has made. God is actively present in his world. He is there creating, recreating, and sustaining. He is in history, shaping, molding, redeeming, and directing events toward the end he has set.

The Psalmist asked: "Whither shall I go from thy Spirit?/Or whither shall I flee from thy presence?" (Ps. 139:7). The answer is nowhere. There is no place one can go in all God's creation and escape God's presence. There are no off limits anywhere in the universe to the creator. There is no nook or corner, no place so dark that one can hide. "Even the darkness is not dark to thee," the psalmist declared, "the night is bright as the day" (Ps. 139:12). God sustains his creation with its myriad forms of life: "When thou takest away their breath, they die/and return to their dust./When thou sendest forth thy Spirit, they are created;/and thou renewest the face of the ground" (Ps. 104:29-30).

It is not surprising then that the Spirit of God is one of the most pervasive realities of the Bible. We meet the Spirit on the first page and on the last. The creation story has scarcely begun when it tells us: "The earth was without form and void, and darkness was upon the face of the deep; and the Spirit of God was moving over the face of the waters" (Gen. 1:2). The Spirit was hovering over a vast, dark, primeval chaos as if to bring order out of it. H. Wheeler Robinson spoke of the Spirit of God as "brooding like a mother-bird upon the face of the waters."

On the last page of the Bible the Spirit gives a winsome invitation of grace: "The Spirit and the Bride say, 'Come.' And let him who hears say, 'Come.' And let him who is thirsty come, let him who desires take the water of life without price" (Rev. 22:17). Between the first and the last, we find the Spirit very active. He gives power to the hero, wisdom to the leader, and vision to the prophet. He was with Jesus of Nazareth, the early preachers, and the new people of God, who are the church.

In the Old Testament, the Spirit, who was something like supernatural energy, was given to Israel's heroes. He made them strong so they could do unusual feats. Samson is a good example. "The Spirit of the Lord came mightily upon him," the narrative tells us, "and he tore the lion asunder as one tears a kid; and he had nothing in his hand" (Judg. 14:6).

Not only did the Spirit of God come upon Israel's heroes but also on her leaders. When Samuel, for example, anointed David to be king of Israel, the Spirit of God came with power on him. "Then Samuel took the horn of oil, and anointed him in the midst of his brothers," the account goes, "and the Spirit of the Lord came mightily upon David from that day forward" (1 Sam. 16:13).

When Israel dreamed of the ideal king, who might be the Messiah, they always envisioned the Spirit of the Lord being on him: "And the Spirit of the Lord shall rest upon him,/the spirit of wisdom and understanding,/the spirit of counsel and might,/the spirit of knowledge and the fear of the Lord" (Isa. 11:2). The same would be true of God's special servant who would have a uniquely redemptive role: "Behold my servant, whom I uphold,/my chosen, in whom my soul delights;/I have put my spirit upon him,/he will bring forth justice to the nations" (Isa. 42:1).

The primary manifestation of the activity of the Spirit in the Old Testament is prophecy. The early prophets, under the influence of the Spirit, often engaged in frenzied, ecstatic, and strange psychological behavior. But this passed when the prophets turned from the ecstatic to the ethical and social pronouncements. The great Hebrew prophets were under the influence of God's Spirit. but they were also involved in the great ethical and social realities of their world. Micah is typical:

> I am filled with power,
> with the Spirit of the Lord,
> and with justice and might,
> to declare to Jacob his transgression
> and to Israel his sin (Mic. 3:8).

In the New Testament we find an even greater emphasis on

the Spirit of God. However, there is not a great emphasis put on the Holy Spirit in the Synoptic Gospels, although Luke says more about him than Matthew and Mark. (The reason for this is likely that the Synoptics do not cover the period when the Spirit was given in abundance—after the death, resurrection, and glorification of Christ.) But they all tell one significant episode of the Spirit: the coming of the Spirit, like a dove, on Jesus at his baptism. This is especially significant when we remember the hope for a new age when God would pour out his chosen Servant in an altogether unparalleled way. This happened at the Jordan River when Jesus was baptized. God gave Jesus his Spirit which endued him with power to go about performing deeds of mercy, healing illnesses, and proclaiming words of salvation.

Matthew and Luke tell of the conception of the virgin Mary by the Holy Spirit which is important in the birth narratives about Jesus.

Luke tells two other incidents about the Spirit which he evidently felt were very significant. Jesus, in his inaugural address in the synagogue at Nazareth, quoted from Isaiah 61:1-2: "The Spirit of the Lord is upon me,/because he has anointed me to preach the good news to the poor" (Luke 4:18).

At the end of his Gospel, Luke makes another important reference to the Holy Spirit: "And behold, I send the promise of my Father upon you; but stay in the city, until you are clothed with power from on high" (Luke 24:49).

When we come to Acts, a very strong emphasis is put on the Holy Spirit. Jesus, the risen Lord, tells his disciples: "But you shall receive power when the Holy Spirit has come upon you; and you shall be my witnesses in Jerusalem and in all Judea and Samaria and to the end of the earth" (Acts 1:8).

It is Acts that tells about the coming of the Spirit at Pentecost just fifty days after the resurrection. The church, a relatively small group of people, waited in prayer and expectancy in Jerusalem. Suddenly the Spirit came upon them "like the rush of a mighty wind" (2:2) from heaven.

There is a real sense in which the Holy Spirit took the place of Jesus. Luke tells us in the sixteenth chapter of Acts that "when they had come opposite Mysia, they attempted to go into Bithynia, but the Spirit of Jesus did not allow them" (v. 7). The Spirit was so much like Jesus that Luke calls him the "Spirit of Jesus."

The great missionary adventure which Acts tells about is under the leadership of the Holy Spirit and is empowered by him. Because of this some scholars believe that Acts should be known, not as The Acts of the Apostles, but as The Acts of the Holy Spirit.

Paul places the same kind of emphasis on the Holy Spirit as does Luke in Acts. There are at least two-hundred fifty references to the Holy Spirit in the New Testament, and at least one-hundred of them are made by Paul. References to the Holy Spirit often crowd each other in his writings. For example, there are nineteen references to the Holy Spirit in the eighth chapter of Romans.

Paul believed that it was the Holy Spirit that makes Christ a living presence in the church. It is the Spirit that gives new life. It is the Holy Spirit that assures us that we are children of God: "It is the Spirit himself bearing witness with our spirit that we are children of God" (Rom. 8:16). It is the Spirit that authenticates, that seals us. We "were sealed with the promised Holy Spirit," Paul tells us (Eph. 1:13). It is the Spirit that takes Christians from diverse ways and backgrounds and welds them into community, giving them unity (1 Cor. 12:13). It is the Spirit that makes possible the radically new life-style of *agape* love. It is the Holy Spirit that pours God's love into our hearts. *Agape* love is the best gift of the Spirit.

When we come to the Johannine literature we find once more a great stress on the Holy Spirit. The Holy Spirit is much more prominent in John's Gospel than in the Synoptics. (The reason for this is likely that John's Gospel was written some twenty years later, which gave him more time to observe the Spirit's working in the life of the church and to reflect on its meaning.)

John saw Jesus uniquely possessing the Spirit. "For he whom God has sent utters the words of God," he wrote, "for it is not by measure that he gives the Spirit" (John 3:34).

John calls the Spirit, whom Jesus would send after his death and resurrection, the Paraclete. At the heart of John's teaching about the Holy Spirit are the four sections which we call the Paraclete sayings (John 14:15-17,25-26; 15:26-27; 16:5-11).

Then there is that marvelous passage in John which tells of Jesus' visit with his disciples on that first Easter night. Jesus greeted them: "Peace be with you." Then he showed them his hands and his side. After a second greeting, Jesus said to them: "As the Father has sent me, even so I send you." Then he breathed on them and said, "Receive the Holy Spirit" (John 20:19,21). This has been called John's Pentecost.

This brief sketch does not, of course, begin to exhaust the teaching about the Holy Spirit in the New Testament, but it does serve to point up the prominence of the Holy Spirit in early Christian experience.

We cannot avoid asking: Is the Spirit of God in the Old Testament and the Holy Spirit in the New Testament the same Spirit? Yes, but two significant differences should be observed. First, the Holy Spirit is like the historic Jesus. Believers could recognize the Holy Spirit because his ministry would be a continuation of the life and teaching of Jesus. He would do and say the things Jesus would do and say. It was as if Jesus had come back in the person of the Holy Spirit. Sometimes a clear distinction is not made between the two. Paul wrote: "For this comes from the Lord who is the Spirit" (2 Cor. 3:18). It is almost as if Paul were saying: "The Lord is the Spirit, and the

Spirit is the Lord." Yet, they were not the same. Second, while the Spirit of God was limited to a few in Israel's life, the Holy Spirit was given to everyone. The Holy Spirit was poured out "upon all flesh." The gift of the Holy Spirit could be spoken of as the democracy of God. The gift was for everyone.

THE HOLY SPIRIT AND PREACHING IN THE NEW TESTAMENT

There can be no doubt that the effectiveness of preaching in the early church was related to the Holy Spirit. The gospel preached by those early preachers was a word of power. Their preaching shook the foundations of two continents. Yet, they were not backed by obvious sources of authority. They were not ambassadors from powerful courts of their world. They represented no gigantic economic interests. They were not spokesmen for powerful ecclesiastical structures. For most part, these preachers were unlearned and unlettered men, Paul being an exception. They went everywhere preaching and their preaching was marked by freedom and spontaneity. As a result of persecution in Jerusalem, the early Christians were scattered. Luke tells us that "those who were scattered went about preaching the word" (Acts 8:4).

One of the historic moments in the early Christian movement was the founding of a church in Antioch, Syria, which was the first church to be planted on Gentile soil. A church there would be free from the limitations of geography. Before it was the vast, sprawling Gentile world. It would be free from the shackling and stifling influence of the parent religion. It would no longer be an appendage to Judaism. This church would become the base for the missionary movement into the Graeco-Roman world. The vitalizing and energizing force in all of this would be the Holy Spirit. "The gift of the Holy Spirit had been poured out even on the Gentiles" (Acts 10:45). This had happened even before the founding of the church at Antioch. The Holy Spirit was very active in the church there. As they worshiped the Lord and were fasting, "the Holy Spirit said, 'Set apart for me Barnabas and Saul for the work to which I have called them'" (Acts 13:2). So the great movement was launched which never stopped until it had penetrated the heart of the Roman empire. What gave these messengers of the radically good news indefatigable strength, courage that was fearless, guidance into strategic centers, and the powerful dynamic of the word they spoke? The Holy Spirit. But had not Jesus promised the power of the Holy Spirit? He had been as good as his word. He had kept his promise.

It is not surprising that D. W. Cleverly Ford has observed: "Preaching then belongs to the dispensation of the Spirit. The era of the Spirit is the era of preaching. The manifestation of the Spirit of God is the foundation of preaching. It is in Pentecost that the origin of preaching must be sought."[1]

The reality of the Holy Spirit in preaching becomes especially obvious when we look at Jesus, Peter, and Paul, the three great preachers of the New Testament.

Luke tells us that after the temptation of Jesus, he "returned in the power of the Spirit into Galilee" (Luke 4:14). He went into Galilee, not in weakness, but in strength. The source of his power was the Holy Spirit. The Holy Spirit that had descended on him at his baptism as a strong presence was now his mighty enabler in his powerful preaching.

While it is Luke who tells us how Jesus began his great Galilean ministry in power, Mark tells us the content of his preaching: "Jesus came into Galilee preaching the gospel of God, and saying, 'The time is fulfilled, and the kingdom of God is at hand; repent, and believe in the gospel'" (Mark 1:14-15). He was announcing good news that was startling indeed. It was a powerful message. They were living through no ordinary time. It was full time, chairos time, time that cannot be measured by watches and calendars. It was creative time. The clock of history was striking, announcing an unusual hour. The kingdom of God, not the kingdom of Rome, was at hand. God was breaking into history in a strange new way, and exercising his reign in a unique way. He was claiming the lives of men and women as never before. Jesus was calling his generation to the only kind of action appropriate for such a crisis hour. They were to repent and believe the good news.

Jesus went into Galilee in the power of the Spirit, preaching a message of power. It was power heaped on power. Is it any wonder the world is still under the spell of his preaching?

Possibly the most powerful sermon in the history of the church was Peter's sermon on the Day of Pentecost. Certainly Peter was not a polished preacher. He was missing in the skills and finesse for which we look in preachers of the modern pulpit. Why his great power? The Holy spirit had come upon him and the church like the rush of a mighty wind.

It was so with Paul. The Holy Spirit more than anything else made him the great preacher he was. A painful memory burned in his mind when he wrote his first letter to the church at Corinth. He recalled his failure when he preached on Mars Hill in Athens. There he had relied too heavily on his rhetorical skills and had tried too hard to accommodate the gospel to the Greek mind. He had quoted their poets and philosophers. Yet, they had scoffed at him. He would never make the same mistake again. He wrote the Corinthians: "And I was with you in weakness and in much fear and trembling; and my speech and my message were not in plausible words of wisdom, but in demonstration of the Spirit and of power" (1 Cor. 2:3-4). We see this man preaching on two continents and releasing forces that would change the course of history. But how did he do it? He told us. He preached in the demonstration of the Spirit and power.

When thinking about the Holy Spirit and preaching in the New Testament, it is important to remember that while the

Holy Spirit produced ecstatic experience such as the speaking in unknown tongues, he did not allow those preachers to make fanciful flights into unreality. Rather the Holy Spirit kept them in touch with reality. He did this essentially in four ways: The Holy Spirit illuminated historical events as God's saving deeds, helped them understand Jesus Christ as the Son of God, produced morality in the lives of believers, and bound the followers of Christ together in community. He kept them in touch with historical reality, spiritual reality, moral reality, and communal reality.

THE HOLY SPIRIT AND PREACHING TODAY

If the Spirit of God were so important to the great prophets of ancient Israel, as well as to the preachers of the early church, we need to recover the meaning of the Holy Spirit for the modern pulpit. Unless we can discover that meaning our preaching will be formal, lifeless, and inept. In determining the function of the Holy Spirit in the preaching for today, we must get our cues from the New Testament.

Let me suggest five ways the Holy Spirit is essential for modern preaching.

First, the Holy Spirit is a forerunner for the preacher. Like John the Baptist preparing the way for the coming of Jesus, the Holy Spirit prepares the way for the spoken word.

The story of Jesus sending the seventy on a mission is told in verse 1 of the tenth chapter of Luke. Jesus "sent them on ahead of him, two by two, into every town and place where he himself was about to come." They would go to the towns and villages that lay along his route, probably making lodging reservation for Jesus as well as other preparations for his coming. In ways more important than that, the Holy Spirit goes ahead of the preacher preparing the way for his coming. This was obviously true of the preaching recorded in the New Testament.

The Holy Spirit came upon the people on Pentecost, breaking down barriers, including language barriers, and creating excitement and expectancy. This happened before and while Peter preached his great sermon. The Holy Spirit had prepared minds and hearts for the reception of Peter's sermon. The Holy Spirit in the hearers was just as important as his presence in the life of the preacher.

Then as Peter preached to a Gentile congregation in Cornelius's house, the Holy Spirit was present and active, helping the hearers to respond to the gospel which Peter was preaching. "The Holy Spirit fell on all who heard the word," the account goes (Acts 10:44). The Holy Spirit was as important to the hearing of the word as he was to the preaching of it.

There is no way of understanding the power of the mission of the early church, led by Paul and others, unless we take into account the Holy Spirit, like a forerunner, going before them and preparing the human soil for the planting of the Word of God. In a world that was like a morally polluted sea, the Holy Spirit created a thirst for moral purity and goodness. In a world where people were increasingly disillusioned with the old gods, the Holy Spirit created a desire for a God like the Father of our Lord and Savior Jesus Christ. In a world where people were burdened with guilt and shame, the Holy Spirit created a longing for peace and forgiveness. In a world that was fragmented and broken, the Holy Spirit created a hunger for wholeness and community that would transcend all barriers that so painfully separated people. In a world where people felt they were caught in revolving doors that went round and round and led nowhere, the Holy Spirit lighted paths of history that led straight into the future, the end of which was an eternal city. The Holy Spirit went before Paul and the other preachers into cities where they would come.

Just so with us. The Holy Spirit prepares the way. Jesus said that "when he comes he will convince the world concerning sin and righteousness and judgment" (John 16:8).

Men and women will not respond to the gospel as good news unless they know the seriousness of their plight, will not gladly receive the offer of forgiveness unless convicted of their sins, will not exult in the freedom and liberation offered unless they understand their bondage, and will not respond to Jesus Christ as Savior and Lord unless they know how lost they are. But who will bring it to pass? The Holy Spirit who goes ahead preparing the soil for the sowing of God's Word.

Second, the Holy Spirit is a presence with us.

If we need somebody to go ahead of us we need somebody to go with us, someone to stand beside us. The pulpit can be a very lonely place. We need a mystical presence there. Such a presence we have in the Holy Spirit.

Jesus promised his frightened disciples a comforter for their unavoidable loneliness. While most things would pass, the Comforter would stay with them forever. "And I will pray the Father," he said, "and he shall give you another Comforter, that he may abide with you for ever" (John 14:16, KJV).

As already noted, the Greek word from which *Comforter* comes is *Paraclete* which literally means one called to your side. It can be translated *counselor, advocate,* or *helper.* It can also mean someone who will stand by you, who will befriend you.

In our weakness, sometimes in our loneliness, as we stand in the pulpit, we can know that the Holy Spirit is with us. He is there to strengthen us, to give us hope, and to energize our frail human words, guiding them to safe lodging in the hearts and minds of the people to whom we preach.

Third, the Holy Spirit plays a vital and important role as interpreter.

The Holy Spirit enlightens us for our hermeneutical task, that of interpreting the Scriptures authentically, yet in such a way that the ancient Word becomes a fresh and contemporary Word. We as preachers have no more crucially important task than that and we cannot do it effectively unless we have the Holy Spirit as interpreter.

D. W. Cleverly Ford has written of the Holy Spirit in this role: "The Spirit, then, is pre-eminently the Interpreter. He is the divine Hermeneut. He opens up the Scripture, he opens up contemporary events in the light of the Scriptures, he opens up the significance of Christ, he opens up the mind, just as the Risen One did on the Emmaus Road. The Spirit makes the hearers of preaching peceive, as did the Risen Christ on the Emmaus Road, the necessity of the cross."[2]

Let me suggest three ways in which the Holy Spirit helps us in our hermeneutical task.

First, he helps us understand the mind of God for us and our time. "For what person knows a man's thoughts except the spirit of the man which is in him?", Paul asked. "So also no one comprehends the thoughts of God except the Spirit of God" (1 Cor. 2:11).

A three-year-old child tells us he has a secret. How can we learn it? Only if the child tells us. Only the spirit of the child knows the mind of the child. If we cannot know the mind of a three-year-old-child unless he tells us, how can we know the mind of God except his Spirit reveals it to us?

We look out upon our world caught in the upheaval and radical change. How shall we know what God is saying in the catastrophic movements of our time? How shall we know where God is acting, where is performing his saving deeds? Who will tell us? Who will throw light on the dark and shadowed landscapes of our time so we can trace God's ways? Only the Holy Spirit.

Again, the Holy Spirit will help us understand the mind of Christ. He will put Jesus Christ into focus. Jesus said of him: "He will teach you all things, and bring to your remembrance all that I have said to you" (John 14:26); "He will bear witness to me" (John 15:26); "He will glorify me, for he will take what is mine and declare it to you" (John 16:14).

The Holy Spirit puts the historic Jesus into a clearer light, and he helps us to understand Christ as our living contemporary. He clarifies the voice of Christ as he speaks to our time. The Holy Spirit does not call attention to himself. He calls attention to Christ. The Holy Spirit stays in the background while keeping Christ in the foreground.

Professor Theo Priess says the Holy Spirit always remains anonymous. He is like a skilled eye surgeon who performs a delicate operation on blind eyes. Before the bandages are removed, the surgeon is gone. One never sees the surgeon, but he sees![3]

Then, the Holy Spirit helps us to hear the ancient Word as a modern Word. But he does more. In some real sense, he transposes the ancient Word into today's life.

We are called to the great but difficult task of speaking the ancient Word so that it becomes a modern Word. But we cannot do it without the Holy Spirit. It is the Holy Spirit that lets us know that the God who has spoken is speaking again.

An old man was seen kneeling before a memorial to William Booth, the founder of the Salvation Army, in a London chapel. His lips moved. He was praying quietly, but fervently: "O God, do it again! Do it again!"

That prayer is often in our hearts, if not on our lips. We want to see God's saving action again, in our time, in our place, and in our lives. Our people need to have that kind of experience when they hear us preach. They want to believe that God is addressing them again; that the deed of grace is being done again, that they are being delivered from bondage again. The Holy Spirit makes it possible.

Fourth, the Holy Spirit helps in realizing the three great tasks of preaching: evangelism, the maturing of believers, and the creating of community.

The ultimate task of evangelism is the creating of new life.

The New Testament makes the staggering claim that we can become new persons in Christ. Paul could speak of our becoming new creations. He knew. That is what had happened to him.

John tells of Jesus confronting the prominent, sophisticated, yet fine, Nicodemus. Jesus startled the famed jurist, now a man of years, when he told him he must be born again. It seemed to defy all rules of reason and experience. Who had ever heard of such a thing? Jesus explained the radical change in terms of the working of the Spirit. "The wind blows where it wills," he said, "and you hear the sound of it, but you do not know whence it comes or whither it goes; so it is with every one who is born of the Spirit" (John 3:8).

It is easy to treat the symptoms of the tragedy of life and not the tragedy itself. We are tempted to settle for putting a little cultural and religious veneer on the old life with its pride, false values, self-centeredness, and alienation. What we need is new life, and only as it is given can our illness be healed and our tragedy overcome. Evangelism must know this, but it is helpless to perform its task without the Holy Spirit.

Once new life has been given, it becomes the task of preaching to help nurture, grow, and mature that new life. Paul has a great deal to say about becoming mature in Christ. Yet, maturity is never clearly defined. Obviously, it had something to do with speaking and doing the truth in love.

Paul, in the twelfth chapter of 1 Corinthians talks about the gifts of the Spirit, and he ends the chapter like this: "And I will show you a still more excellent way." The more excellent way is the gift of the Spirit and is the way of Christian love. Paul describes this way in the thirteenth chapter of 1 Corinthians. As we read this chapter we feel Paul is describing Jesus, the one fully mature person. We are called to that kind of maturity, but it is only through the gifts of the Spirit that we grow into a maturity that resembles Jesus.

The Holy Spirit also aids preaching in creating a community

which overcomes the barriers thrown up by people in their sin and pride. The new life needs a community of love and acceptance, for only in such a community can it grow and reach maturity.

The ancient world, like ours, was very hostile and divided. Great cultural, economic, political, religious, and sexual chasms lay across it, fragmenting and dividing it. Yet, miracle of miracles, these barriers were overcome in the church, and Paul saw the Spirit playing a significant role in this. "For by one Spirit we were all baptized into one body—Jews or Greeks, slaves or free—and all were made to drink of one Spirit" (1 Cor. 12:13).

All too frequently the modern church reflects the barriers, social stratification, and fragmentation of our world. How can such a church speak the saving word to its broken and fragmented world? How can such a church bring to maturity those within its life? It can't. It must become a community of love, grace, and acceptance that transcends the brokenness of divisions of the world before it can. But it will become such a community only as the Holy Spirit heals and empowers it. Let preaching know this, and let it use the resources which the Spirit makes available.

Fifth, the Holy Spirit can empower preaching.[4]

The Spirit of God is many things, but maybe he is power more than anything else.

One of the most significant and dramatic chapters of the Bible is the thirty-seventh chapter of Ezekiel. The prophet stood overlooking an ancient battlefield. Neither the vanquisher nor the vanquished had removed their dead from the battlefield. The only reminder of that battle was the bones of the men who had died there. There they were—bleached bones on desert sands. There was not a stir of life to be seen anywhere. Nothing is so dead as bleached bones on desert sand. As Ezekiel looked out on that desolate scene, God asked him: "Son of man, can these bones live?" It all seemed so impossible. The prophet answered: "O Lord God, thou knowest" (v. 3). At the command of God, Ezekiel prophesied to those bones. Then there was a mighty rattling across the desert valley as bones came together to form skeletons. Flesh came upon the skeletons and skin covered the flesh. There they were, perfectly formed bodies, but lifeless. A mighty wind swept across the valley, and God breathed his breath into those dead forms. And they lived, standing to their feet as a mighty host. Only the Spirit of God had power enough to bring life out of that lifeless situation.

The Spirit of God gives power, and preaching in the New Testament, as has already been said, is aware of this. As Luke brings his Gospel to a close, Jesus was looking at his disciples, who were not an imposing group, saying to them: "You are witnesses of these things. And behold, I send the promise of my Father upon you; but stay in the city, until you are clothed with power from on high" (Luke 24:48-49). And they did wait—for fifty days. Then the Holy Spirit came upon them with mighty power, turning their weakness into strength. The early preachers were startled by the power of their words. But one thing they knew: They went not in their own strength but in the power of the Holy Spirit.

The modern pulpit needs badly to know that power again. The pulpit is supposed to be a place of power, but often it is not. It frequently is a place of weakness and ineffectiveness. How often those of us who stand there are tired. We labor beneath the burden of preaching. There is no answer to our problem apart from the Holy Spirit.

Many a pastor on a blue Monday, remembering the trudging gait of his preaching the day before, has asked: "Lord God, can the pulpit live?" And God answers: "Yes, if the winds of God blow over it and if the Holy Spirit is on him who stands there."

We are often like sailboats that do not sail. No wind is blowing. But we can unfurl our sails against the sky and wait for the winds, believing that they will blow again. Or we are like barges beached on the sand. We feel we have priceless cargo on board, but we cannot move. We are stuck in the sand. Only the incoming tide of the Spirit can lift and move us. But we may be sure that the tide will come in again.

The Holy Spirit is not ours. It is God's and it is his to give. We cannot manipulate God nor set schedules for his gift of the Spirit. He will give it when, where, and to whom he will. But we can wait, hope, and pray for the gift, believing that God will not fail us, and with the gift we shall receive power.

8
Preaching That Has Authority

Most people do not want their pastor to be authoritarian, but they do want him to be authoritative. While resisting heavy-handedness in the pulpit, they want to be confronted with the truth—truth that springs from the heart of reality, truth that lays hold of their lives, claiming them. They want truth which they cannot deny, truth with which they do not want to argue. This does not mean they will not resist the truth when it judges their false personal and social values, but in their best moments they know they cannot be who they should be until they have yielded to the truth. As the pastor preaches they should feel authority in him.

An accomplished violinist who played under Toscanini told us that as soon as the great conductor mounted the rostrum the orchestra felt the authority of the man flowing over them. There should be something of that quality in the person who stands in the pulpit.

What will enable us to preach with authority? That is a question we should wrestle with.

AUTHORITY OF GOD'S WORD

A preacher finds his or her ultimate authority in God's Word. Indeed he cannot be authoritative unless he proclaims the Word of God. It is this Word that makes the sermon unique.

"Give the words their strict meaning as address is a man talking to men," wrote William E. Sangster. "A sermon is a man speaking from God. The authority of the preacher, unlike that of a speaker, is not in himself: He is a herald. His word is not his own; it comes from above."[1]

Andrew W. Blackwood, for many years professor of preaching at Princeton Theological Seminary, said that Charles Haddon Spurgeon was the greatest preacher since Paul. Spurgeon knew well that we are saved by a word from beyond ourselves and that it is that word we must speak from the pulpit. Spurgeon as a boy of fifteen was driven from the streets of London one Sunday morning into a wayside Methodist chapel by a blinding snowstorm. The weather was so severe that the pastor had not been able to get there, and a lay leader was in charge of the service. Spurgeon remembered that he was a poor preacher, but had a great text which he repeated over and over again: "Look unto me, and be ye saved, all the ends of the earth: for I am God, and there is none else" (Isa. 45:22, KJV). Spurgeon was greatly moved by the truth of the text, and at the end of the service he turned by faith to the great God of our universe, who looks upon his whole creation with love, and was saved.

A minister asked Robert J. McCracken, who was then pastor of the Riverside Church, New York City, why people come to church. On the face of it, it seems to be a silly question, but in fact is very important. Why do people keep coming to church Sunday after Sunday, month after month, and year after year? The church, more than other institutions, draws people consistently in rather large numbers on a voluntary basis. McCracken thought for a moment and said: "They came hoping to hear a word from beyond them."

King Zedekiah during a great national crisis sent for Jeremiah who was in prison and asked: "Is there any word from the Lord?" (Jer. 37:17). That is the question so many people are asking as they come to church. Here is a young person for whom life is like a jigsaw puzzle whose pieces do not fit together. He is asking: "Is there a word from God that makes sense out of life?" Here is a woman in a deep depression. The shadow over her mind has been heavy for weeks. She is asking: "Is there a word of hope from God which can lift this shadow that threatens to destroy me?" Here is a man whose evil ways have wrecked his life. He feels so guilty and wretched. He is asking: "Is there a word of forgiveness from God that can give me a new life?" Here is an old man who has shuffled to church this morning. The question of death has long ceased to be an academic matter. He expects to meet it any day now, and he is asking: "Is there life beyond death?"

The preacher takes heart in knowing that God has spoken, that God has given his word in such a way that he can hear it and speaks it. He knows his greatest task and highest privilege is to speak God's word to his people. His greatest concern will be that he speak that word with clarity and power.

What are the dimensions of this word we are to speak? I am suggesting four—personal, ethical, social, and corporate.

I want God's word to be personal. I don't want to be lost in the faceless mass of humanity. I am sure God has named all things in his universe, but I want him to know my name. I want to be like Paul who could say of Christ that he "loved me and gave himself for me" (Gal. 2:20). I am glad that God loves his whole creation, but I want to know that he loves me. I know there is enough grace in Christ to cover the sins of the world, but I want to know that he has forgiven my sin.

The word of God does not disappoint me. It is indeed personal. It touches the deepest, most interior springs of my life. It calls me by name.

Do you remember that the towering personalities of the Bible felt that God had addressed them personally? Moses on the back side of a desert, standing before a burning bush that was not consumed, heard God calling him, "Moses, Moses!" (Ex. 3:4). Isaiah, in his great Temple experience, recounted how a seraphim took a burning coal from the altar and touched his lips and said: "Behold, this has touched your lips; your guilt is taken away, and your sin forgiven" (Isa. 6:7). Amos remembered how God confronted him when he was with his herds and said to him, "Go, prophesy to my people Israel" (Amos 7:15). Jeremiah in describing his commission to be a prophet said God "put forth his hand and touched my mouth; and the Lord said to me, 'Behold, I have put my words in your mouth'" (Jer. 1:9). It was so personal. Saul, with his face in the dust along the Damascus road heard Christ addressing him: "Saul, Saul, why do you persecute me?" (Acts 9:4).

The word of God is not only personal, it is ethical. It is concerned with motivation, behavior, values, and relationships.

Christians seem to have been first called those of "the Way." (See Acts 9:2; 19:9,23; 22:4; 24:14,22). While we would not be dogmatic in claiming to know the meaning of the epithet, it likely indicated a practical way of life as contrasted to a speculative and ethereal kind of religion. The ethical element in the Christian life was strong from the very beginning.

Yet, the strong emphasis in the ethical was never legalistic. Two things kept it from being that: the gospel of grace and the dynamics of the Holy Spirit working in the ethical life.

We are not saved by good works, as in legalism. We do not bring a handful of virtues to God. We bring empty hands, and he saves us anyway because his salvation is of grace. Good works are not the roots of salvation, as in legalism, they are the fruits of salvation by grace.

Also, we do not have to bear the ethical load in our strength. There is the power of the Holy Spirit working in us to achieve ethical ends. Paul writes about the fruits of the Spirit, and, surprisingly enough, they are ethical in nature. Love is the chief fruit which the Spirit bears. What if we had to realize in our own strength the kind of love seen in Jesus? It would be an impossibility, a burden no one could carry. We don't have to bear it! "God's love has been poured into our hearts through the Holy Spirit which has been given to us," Paul tells us (Rom. 5:5).

Jesus Christ is our model and we are to desire his quality of life which is *agape* love. We are to "walk in love, as Christ loved us and gave himself up for us, a fragrant offering and sacrifice to God" (Eph. 5:2). We should remember that this love is non-manipulative, nonutilitarian, and nonpossessive. It does not use people, does not demean them, and does not turn them into things and tools. It is a love that serves and gives itself away. It loves not only the beautiful, the strong, the healthy, and the good. It loves the weak, the sickly, the ugly, the marred, and the sinful.

Love is social by its very nature. To love in the Christian sense is to love somebody. Therefore, the word of God which we preach is social in nature. We are to be concerned with the brother, with the neighbor.

The two basic poles in the Christian faith are God and the neighbor. We are to love both. Paul saw the Commandments being fulfilled essentially in love and concern for the neighbor. In one of the greatest ethical sections of the New Testament, Paul writes: "Owe no one anything, except to love one another; for he who loves his neighbor has fulfilled the law. The commandments, 'You shall not commit adultery, You shall not kill, You shall not steal, You shall not covet,' and any other commandment, are summed up in this sentence, 'You shall love your neighbor as yourself.' Love does no wrong to a neighbor; therefore love is the fulfilling of the law" (Rom. 13:8-10).

We can't make it alone, and we don't have to. There are fellow travelers who go with us. In life's most solitary moment we can hear the shuffling of feet. A brother goes there. There are many feet. Many go with us. We need to love and care for them the way Jesus did.

Finally, the word of God is corporate in nature. It addresses the life we live together. It calls for involvement. It demands justice, compassion, and humaneness in our world.

This is the word we hear most poorly. We are content with a more personal, even more private religion. We often want to hear only the personal word. We like things more spiritual. We like burning hearts, ecstasy, and spiritual highs. We had rather not get involved in setting things right in our social structures, in our corporate life. The demands of justice are too hard, its pursuits are too painful. Yet, God calls us there.

I have talked about God personally addressing the great personalities of the Bible. But it is very important to make this observation: It mattered not how warm, intimate, and personal the experience, God normally called the person to the corporate life. It was from the personal encounter to corporate task. God addressed Moses by name, only to send him into Egypt to deliver his people who were slaves. He touched Isaiah's lips with forgiving grace and then sent him to a hardhearted, rebellious people. God confronted Amos in a very personal way and directed him to the Northern Kingdom of Israel. God put his word on Jeremiah's lips and then sent him to nations and kingdoms. The living Christ called Saul by name, only to commission him as apostle to the vast, sprawling Gentile world.

Let us be grateful that God's word is first of all personal. There is no forgiveness and new life unless we are personally addressed by God. But let us not forget that the personal word leads to the corporate task.

THE AUTHORITY OF PERSONAL REALITY

The crowds who heard Jesus found his authority fresh, arresting and spontaneous. They said that "he taught them as one who had authority, and not as their scribes" (Matt. 7:29).

What was the difference between the authority of the scribes and the authority of Jesus? The scribes were always quoting ancient sources and old traditions. Their authority was borrowed, secondhand, and external. But how different with Jesus! He didn't feel the necessity to quote anybody, not even the best authorities. His authority overflowed from the inward reality of his own life. George Buttrick has written: "The scribes drew stale water from closed cisterns. But the words of Jesus were like a spring, clear, fresh, with power to slake the soul's thirst."[2] The scribes were like men priming old pumps while Jesus was like an artesian well. Jesus' authority was inward and personal. While the preacher's authority can never be as final and ultimate as Jesus', it must be of the same kind. It must come from personal reality. It, too, must be inward, personal, spontaneous.

The New Testament puts such a strong emphasis on personal and experiential authority. Jesus said to Nicodemus: "Truly, truly, I say to you, we speak of what we know, and bear witness to what we have seen" (John 3:11). The people of Sychar, who having been fascinated by the testimony of the Samaritan woman and following her to Jacob's well to see Jesus, said to her: "It is no longer because of your words we believe, for we have heard for ourselves, and we know that this is indeed the Savior of the world" (John 4:42). A blind man whom Jesus had healed on the Sabbath, resisting the Pharisees who claimed that Jesus was a sinner exclaimed, "Whether he is a sinner, I do not know; one thing I know, that though I was blind, now I see" (John 9:25). John began his first epistle like this: "That which was from the beginning, which we have heard, which we have seen with our eyes, which we have looked upon and touched with our hands, concerning the word of life—the life was made manifest, and we saw it, and testify to it, and proclaim to you the eternal life which was with the Father and· was made manifest to us—that which we have seen and heard we proclaim also to you" (1 John 1:1-3).

Anyone who would be really effective in the pulpit must

have an authority which is inward and personal in nature. Jeremiah, envisioning a new covenant, heard God say: "I will put my law within them, and I will write it upon their hearts; and I will be their God, and they shall be my people" (Jer. 31:33). Paul could speak of "Christ who lives in me" (Gal. 2:20).

God's great saving events, such as the Exodus and the coming of Christ, are objective. They are as objective as a range of mountains, and how I feel about them does not change them at all. But I must let God do inside me what he has done outside me. The objective must become subjective. I must let the grace that was in Christ become grace in me, the forgiveness that was in Christ become forgiveness in me, the compassion that was in Christ become compassion in me, the acceptance that was in Christ become acceptance in me, and the love that was in Christ become love in me. I must let the freedom that Christ achieved in his death and resurrection become freedom for me. I must know the freedom from enslaving sin. I must know the freedom from death which Christ makes possible for me in his gift of eternal life, and I must never forget the nature of that eternal life which lies in a new relationship with God which can never be broken. When this has happened to me, there is some basic sense in which I can say "Christ lives in me." Then I can speak with authority.

I am talking about a kind of incarnation. I enflesh the truth of Christ, the gospel he brings. Yet, it should be clearly said that this incarnation is not possible in a life that is essentially private. It cannot take place in isolation. It must not be so mystical that we are not in touch with the common realities of life. This incarnation takes place in relationship with people and our world. For example, I cannot incarnate the love of Christ unless I love somebody, nor his compassion unless I am compassionate to somebody, nor his acceptance unless I accept somebody. I cannot incarnate the suffering of Christ unless I suffer with and for people. I have to live where Christ lived—among men.

David H. C. Read has written of the importance of this incarnation in preaching. "The sermon constructed in the isolation booth could be theologically immaculate," he wrote, "structurally perfect, thoroughly biblical, beautifully illustrated, logically impeccable—yet a total failure as an instrument of the Word of God. Why? Because it lacks incarnation; it has never been earthed in the experience of the preacher with the people to whom he speaks. The man 'sent from God' is not a hermit conceiving his oracles in isolation from the passions, the joys, the sorrow of Tom, Dick and Harry, and delivering them from his private Sinai. He is sent right into the world to know at first hand and to be vulnerable to every tremor of his neighbor's pain and joy. That is why the Word of God can be heard in the stumbling words and technically inadequate sermon of a parish minister who really knows and loves his flock, and perhaps not at all in the polished discourse of the cloistered scholar."[3]

We would do well to heed St. Francis of Assisi's motto for preaching: "Unless you preach everywhere you go, there is no use to go anywhere to preach." We certainly can't preach everywhere we go unless the gospel lives in us.

THE AUTHORITY OF SERVANTHOOD

Jesus was a servant, and the preacher is not better than his Lord. The fact that Jesus was a servant did not in any way diminish his authority. Rather it enhanced it. Just so with the preacher. As a servant he or she embodies the realities of humility, love, and ministry in a way not possible in any other role. Obviously this makes for authority, but this does not exhaust the possibilities of the preacher's authority in the pulpit.

The preacher is called to speak a word not his own. He speaks for everybody else. "What we preach is not ourselves," Paul wrote, "but Jesus Christ as Lord, with ourselves as your servant for Jesus' sake" (2 Cor. 4:5).

We are called to speak God's word. As servants we do not

obtrude, we do not get in the way of the word we speak. We do not call attention to ourselves but to the word. In a sense, we speak the word and then step aside so it can be fully and freely released. We do not stand in its path. Therefore we speak with authority because we do not hamper an authority of which we are not the source. We become its mouthpiece, its vehicle.

Yet, we are most sorely tempted not to be servants. We can well listen to J. H. Jowett: "I strongly believe the artisan who works with his hands, or the trader who is busy in commerce, or the professional man who labours in law, or in medicine, or in literature, or in music, or art, is not able to conceive the insidious and deadly perils which infest the life of a minister."[4]

It may be that the pulpit is the place where we are most greatly tempted. There we are more the center of things than anywhere else. We can be like an actor on the stage with the spotlights turned on us. Our people can be a captive audience that we manipulate to our glory. We can so easily be master and not servant in the pulpit.

We should be like John the Baptist who "came for testimony, to bear witness to the light, that all might believe through him. He was not the light, but came to bear witness to the light" (John 1:7-8). We should be willing to decrease that Jesus might increase. We are not in the pulpit to call attention to ourselves but to him. We are a messenger crying, "make straight the way of the Lord." We are a hand pointing and a voice exclaiming, "Behold, the Lamb of God!"

Anything that would turn us from a witness of Christ to a witness to ourselves is indeed most dangerous. It is easy for pride, ambition, ability, or gifts to obtrude, to get between us and him so that our vision of him becomes blurred and our voice that would speak of him becomes weak and faint. William E. Sangster has warned us: "The preacher has his own temptation to pride, and everything that keeps him low before God is to be welcomed."[5]

I can remember as a boy how Baptist people in eastern North Carolina used to pray for their pastor just before he preached: "O God, hide our pastor behind the cross and let us not see him but Jesus." That prayer was repeated over and over again but it never lost its meaning because it spoke of such important things.

J. H. Jowett remembered preaching at a camp meeting near Northfield, Massachusetts. His congregation consisted of men from the Water Street Mission in New York. Just before he preached a man prayed: "O Lord, we thank Thee for our brother. Now blot him out! Reveal Thy glory to us in blazing splendour that he shall be forgotten." Jowett, on reflection of the prayer, said: "It was absolutely right and I trust the prayers were answered."[6]

Robert J. McCracken told an incident from H. G. Wood's biography of T. R. Glover, the scholar and public orator of Cambridge University. Glover was on vacation at Sheringhan and was attending, along with several other distinguished scholars, the Primitive Methodist Chapel there. It was Easter and a local preacher, who was old but highly esteemed in the town, was preaching that morning. The old man began by telling his congregation that he had asked one of his distinguished guests to preach, but being refused he had to do it himself. "Now," he said, "you musn't think about the man who is giving you bread, but about the bread itself." This greatly moved Rendel Harris who slapped Glover on the knee and said: "That's the best thing I have heard about preaching—not the man who gives it, but the bread iteslf."[7]

A story is told about St. Francis who was once applauded by his fellows at the close of his sermon. He went home in tears and repented because men had applauded him rather than bowing in reverence at the feet of his Lord.

Being a servant in the pulpit doesn't mean we are to be timid, apologetic, or self-effacing. It doesn't mean we fail to achieve or sacrifice excellence. Indeed, we seek to realize the finest possible excellence in terms of scholarship, homiletical skill, use of language, style, and speaking ability. But it does mean that we press our excellence into the service of the word we have been called to preach.

Commitment to servanthood in the pulpit will answer many questions about preaching. For example, what about humor in the pulpit? Humor can lighten a very heavy, plodding sermon. Yet, it can be very dangerous. The preacher can become more an entertainer than a minister of the word. Preaching can degenerate into the trivial, even the absurd, when humor is irresponsibly used. But humor has a legitimate place when it is pressed into the service of the Word. It is not humor for humor's sake. It is humor for the Word's sake.

What about sarcasm and irony in the pulpit? Like humor, they can be dangerous. When a preacher uses them too often or in the wrong spirit, they may stifle the love and compassion that people should sense in him, leaving him harsh, derisive, and self-righteous. But sarcasm and irony have great power, and can expose evil in subtle ways that may be more effective than a direct assault on it. While being very dangerous when misused, they have a proper and legitimate place in the pulpit. The rule is: They must be the servant of the Word.

What about style? A preacher should be a master of language out of which he fashions style. He should use the kind of language the Bible does—vivid, concrete, picturesque. Biblical language has an earthy quality, a kind of salty tang. His style should have clarity, beauty, and force as well as other qualities. Yet, his words must be the servant of the word. It is not style for style's sake. It is style for the word's sake.

We must not forget that Christ has called us to be

servants. We cannot be ministers of his unless we are, and nowhere should we be more sensitively aware of this than in the pulpit. To be true to this calling should be the consuming ambition of our lives, and the temptation that would turn us aside should be feared as a deadly thing as indeed it is. We shall be strengthened in knowing that in losing our lives as servants of Christ, we shall find them.

The modern pulpit needs many things but likely nothing more than the recovery of authority. One of our most urgent tasks should be that of making preaching authoritative. Until it is, the pulpit cannot be engaging and arresting.

9
Preaching That Is in Touch with Life

In the last chapter we were concerned with authority in preaching. The preacher finds his authority in proclaiming the Word of God, experiencing that Word, and being its servant. But he must make sure that his preaching is in touch with life. His preaching should be both authoritative and relevant.

A preacher may be in touch with the Word of God but not with his people. He may be a good biblical scholar and theologian but not be sensitive to the needs of people. He may keep the Word of God but lose his people. But why preach if we miss our people? On the other hand, a preacher may keep his people and lose the Word. He may be aware of his world with its questions, moods, values, hope, and pains. He may know science, psychology, sociology, history, politics, and other subjects, but not be grounded in biblical thought. Yet, why preach if one really does not have a word from God? A preacher who knows only the Word of God is like a person firing a highly powerful rifle without aiming, while a preacher who knows only his people is like a marksman, carefully zeroed in on his target but firing blank cartridges.

In this chapter we are concerned with relating the gospel to people. We must be very sensitive to those who hear us. We must be able to read the hope and pain in the faces of those who sit before us. We must make sure that the word we speak is the

Word of God and that it reaches them.

We should remember a very basic truth: In effective preaching, a people-oriented word is preached through a person to people. It is so simple that it may sound trite, yet it is not. It comes to the heart of the preaching task.

A PEOPLE-ORIENTED WORD

The Word of God is people oriented. The Bible is a story about God seeking men and women, finding them, and addressing them. We are tempted to interpret the Bible as people seeking and addressing God. But that is to misunderstand the biblical story.

Remember the two simple but profound questions asked by God that are recorded in the early chapters of Genesis? After Adam and Eve had sinned and in their guilt and shame were trying to hide from God among the trees of the Garden, God asked: "Where are you?" (Gen. 3:9). Then came the first murder. A brother killed a brother, and God confronted Cain, the murderer, with a very direct and poignant question: "Where is Abel your brother?" (Gen. 4:9).

Those two questions, while simple are very profound. The first one asked: What is your relationship with God? That is the primal question. It is spiritual in nature. The second question asked: What is your relationship with your brother? It is social in nature and very important, also. It is not surprising that these two questions came hard upon each other. They belong together, and you really can't ask one without asking the other. You can't be right with God and wrong with your brother, and you can't be wrong with God and right with your brother. It would be cruelly tantalizing if the Bible asked these two questions and did not answer them. The Bible is untiring in telling how God has answered them, and his supreme effort was a radical, daring, and sacrificial one. The cross of Jesus Christ is the answer to both. "For if while we were enemies we were reconciled to God by the death of his Son," Paul wrote, "much more, now that we are reconciled, shall we be saved by his life" (Rom. 5:10). We are reconciled to God by the cross of Jesus and that is the way we are reconciled to our estranged brothers.

The cross is the way God reconciled Jew and Gentile, so hostile and separated. He took this radical action so "that he might create in himself one new man in place of the two, so making peace, and might reconcile us both to God in one body through the cross, thereby bringing the hostility to an end" (Eph. 2:15-16). If God could reconcile Jew and Gentile, es-tranged people everywhere can take hope.

The Incarnation tells how people oriented the Word of God is. "And the Word became flesh and dwelt among us," John tells us, "full of grace and truth; we have beheld his glory, glory as of the only Son from the Father" (John 1:14). The Word did not dwell above us, or away from us, not even beside us. The Word dwelt among us.

Jesus in his inaugural address, recorded in the fourth chapter of Luke, made it clear that his word was not an abstract, speculative, or ethereal word. It was about people and spoken to people in dire need. It was a word of hope to the poor, the captives, the blind, and the oppressed. It was a word to those who waited for Jubilee with its rest, freedom, restoration of property, and new beginnings.

Remember when John the Baptist, whose faith had been so strong and certain, wavered, coming under a shadow of doubt? It was one thing to believe along the sunlit banks of the Jordan River with great crowds hanging on every word he spoke. But it was another thing to believe in a dark, damp prison cell, cut off from disciples and friends who loved and supported him. In that prison cell John wondered if Jesus were really the Messiah, whose way he had prepared. He sent Jesus a message: "Are you he who is to come, or shall we look for another?" (Matt. 11:3). Jesus replied: "Go and tell John what you hear and see: the blind receive their sight and the lame walk, lepers are cleansed and the deaf hear, and the dead are raised up, and the poor have good news preached to them" (Matt. 11:4-5). The proof that he was the Messiah was what was happening to people. The promises of his inaugural address, so people oriented, were being fulfilled.

When a preacher prepares his sermon, with one eye on the Bible and an eye on his people, he makes a wonderful discovery: The great themes of the Bible move to people the way a stream flows to the sea.

The word we preach touches human life at the points of real need. It is judgment—God's judgment—to people in their evil and shame, forgiveness to the guilty, and reconciliation to those who are estranged from God and separated from their brothers. It is redemption and freedom to those who are enslaved, light to those in darkness, and hope to those in despair. It is assurance to the frightened, peace to the anxious, strength to the weak, and the way home to the lost. It is foundation to the insecure, an anchor to those adrift, and the power that lifts to their feet those who have gone down in defeat. It is height, wonder, and mystery to those whose lives have been flattened out, purpose to those who are bereft of meaning, worth to those who feel cheap, and fixed points for those who are confused by changing landscapes. It is the gift of a presence to those who are alone, the fellowship of the people of God to the uprooted, the family of God to the homeless. It is a face filled with the light of God to those who find religion vague and obscure, love as the way to those whose moral signs are blurred, and grace to those who are under the pride and guilt of legalism. It is healing to the broken, life to the dying, and the assurance that "nothing can separate us from the love of God" to those who know how fragile the most precious relations of life are.

THROUGH A PERSON

This people-oriented word is preached through a person. You will note that I did not say by a person, but through a person. The preacher may be nothing more than a mouthpiece when it is spoken by him. But for the gospel to be spoken through him means he has become the channel for the Word of God. As a mouthpiece, he may speak it fluently without any great depth or conviction. But to be a channel for the gospel is another matter. In some real sense the preacher has become a part of the gospel and the marks of his life are on it. The gospel is something that has happened to him. It has become good news for him, and, because it has, he is sure that it can be good news to those who hear him.

When the gospel passes through you, you affirm it with your mind, you believe in its veracity and truthfulness, you accept its credibility. But that is not enough. You experience it with your heart. Your heart glows over it. You can say with those disciples who walked with the risen Lord along the Emmaus road: "Did not our hearts burn within us while he talked to us on the road, while he opened to us the scriptures?" (Luke 24:31).

John Wesley, in recalling his Aldersgate experience, said his heart was strangely warmed. It is no wonder that the gospel he preached after that had such warmth and power. Wesley knew what it was for his heart to glow over the gospel he preached.

Not only do our minds affirm the gospel we preach and our hearts glow over it, but we translate it into life. This we do with our will. The gospel is something we do. We give voice, hands, and feet to it. We clothe it with life.

What kind of person makes the best channel for the gospel? A thoroughly human person, who is loving and caring, and who is in touch with people.

We are not little gods perched behind pulpits. We are not angels with seraphs' songs. Thank God we are not. How could an angel, who has not known sin, tell of the grace of forgiveness? How could a divinity who does not know the certainty and pain of death exult in the resurrection of Jesus?

Paul could say: "We have this treasure in earthen vessels" (2 Cor. 4:7). We have our gospel, not in heavenly vessels but in earthen vessels, not in perfect vessels but in human ones.

When Paul and Barnabas came to Lystra on their first missionary journey, the natives thought they were gods. They said: "The gods have come down to us in the likeness of men!" (Acts 14:11). Paul and Barnabas responded quickly and urgently. "Men, why are you doing this?" they asked. "We also are men, of like nature with you, and bring you good news, that you should turn from these vain things to a living God who made the heaven and the earth and the sea and all that is in them" (Acts 14:15). Just so with us. We should, in and out of the pulpit, try to tell people in many ways: "We are men and women of like nature with you and bring you good news."

Gardner C. Taylor, reminiscing about the black preachers he had heard as a boy in Louisiana, says this about them: "They would say in their picturesque way, their voices now rolling like thunder, now whispering like the sighing of the wind in the trees: 'God might have found so many other ways to spread the Gospel of the love of God. He might have written His love on the leaves of trees and the blowing winds would have sent news of deliverance and redemption far and wide. God might have written his love in the skies and in the rising sun so that men, looking upward could read the message, God so loved the world. He might have made the ocean sing His love and nightingales to chant it, neither of these, nor even angels, could ever preach and say, however, I've been redeemed. So this is a Gospel for sinners saved by grace, and only saved sinners can preach.' This old eloquence touches the heart of the matter."[1]

A preacher who is a channel of the gospel must love people. If he does not, how can he preach effectively the superlative love the world has seen in Jesus Christ?

Phillips Brooks is considered by many to be the greatest preacher America has produced. In 1942 I visited Trinity Church in Boston where Brooks was rector for twenty-two years. At the time of my visit, one of the finest preachers of the American pulpit, Theodore F. Ferris, was rector of the church. Ferris had a very fine sermon that morning, but I was distracted. I kept thinking of Phillips Brooks, and I imagined him, big of body and spirit, as he once stood in that pulpit preaching one of his great sermons. But the really significant thing that day happened after the service was over, while I was on the church lawn looking at a statue of Brooks. The statue of Brooks is life-size, and is standing within a portico beneath a half-dome. He is beside the pulpit with his left arm resting on it. His right hand is raised as if he were about to speak. Towering above him is the living Christ whose right hand is resting on Brooks' left shoulder. It is as if Christ were saying to him: "Go ahead, Brooks, and speak the Word, I am with you to empower you." Carved on the pedestal is this inscription: "Phillips Brooks—Preacher of the Word of God, Lover of Mankind." Many things have been said about him but these two are enough. Brooks could never have been the great preacher he was unless he had loved people the way he did. He cared intensely for the pastoral side of the ministry.

The effective preacher must care about others. He must be concerned about the total life of persons and care enough to identify with them. Their frustration and pain as well as their hope and joy must become his own.

Job could say of himself: "I was eyes to the blind,/and feet to the lame./I was a father to the poor,/and I searched out the cause of him whom I did not know" (Job 29:15-16). Job could be a good example for us who preach. He did not keep a safe distance from people. He stepped across the line that would have been forbidding to many and took into his own life the pain and privation of others.

When Saul met the resurrected Lord along the Damascus road, Christ said to him, "Saul, Saul, why do you persecute me?" (Acts 9:4). Saul could have easily remonstrated: "I don't understand, Lord. I have never seen you. Although we were contemporaries, we lived far apart. I never met you. It is true that I persecuted your followers, but I never laid a lash on you." Christ could talk that way because he was fully identified with those who believed in and followed him. When they were whipped, he was beaten. When they were arrested, he was taken into custody. When they were put in jail, he was behind prison bars. Their pain and anguish were his own. Christ is our model.

Clyde E. Fant, Jr., and William M. Pinson, Jr., in surveying great preaching across twenty centuries have this to say in their preface: "The sermons in this study demonstrate the relevance with which these men preached to the specific needs of people and the issues of their day. Not one of them was lost in abstract theology, aimless piety, or ranting exhortation. There is no artificial division in their preaching between ethics and evangelism. The essential fact is they cared. They cared about people, their pain and grief—whether spiritual, physical, moral, or social—and they addressed themselves to that."[2]

The preacher who is an effective channel for God's Word will be in touch with people. He will live among them.

Mention has been made of the greatness of Phillips Brooks as a preacher. One of the sources of his greatness was that he never lost the common touch with people. He intensely loved the pastoral side of the Christian ministry. He visited from home to home almost every day. He stayed in contact with as many of his parish as he possibly could, and he was in touch with many who lived beyond his parish. He often confessed that he could not preach unless he maintained the personal touch with people.

It has been said of Dick Sheppard, the great English preacher: "In him, more than in any other preacher in our time, the new glory of the pulpit is illustrated—not the glory of sublime oratory or profound thought, but the greater glory of the man who stands in the midst of people, a friend and brother, pouring out his soul in the passion of service and love."[3]

Time magazine selected E. V. Hill, pastor of the Mt. Zion Missionary Baptist Church in Los Angeles as one of its seven star preachers of Protestantism. It had this, among other things, to say about him. "It is clear that he is down there, an Everyman in the street, wrestling with the devil himself."[4] Here is one of the secrets of his greatness. He lives among people. He is in touch with them.

TO PEOPLE

The preacher must realize that he is to reach people with his message. It matters not how faithful he is to the Bible or how accurate he is in his exegetical work, he is a failure in the pulpit if the truth he preaches does not find lodging in the minds and hearts of those who hear him. The preacher in preparing a sermon should keep before him a text and human faces. There faces will be familiar since they are of his own congregation. Which is more important, the text or the faces? That is a hard question to answer, but if either is neglected the sermon will be a failure.

Alexander Maclaren, for forty-four years a pastor in Manchester, England, and one of the greatest expositors in the history of preaching, always placed across from him an empty chair and imagined a person sitting there as he prepared his sermon. While Maclaren worked on his sermon, a dialogue went on between him and the imaginary person. That chair kept him from forgetting that he would be preaching to people Sunday morning, and he would keep them before him as he made preparation.

J. W. Jowett shared his method of keeping his sermon people oriented. "When I have got my theme clearly defined and I begin to prepare its exposition," he wrote, "I keep in the circle of my mind at least a dozen men and women, very varied in their natural temperaments, and very dissimilar in their daily circumstances. They are not abstractions, neither are they dolls or dummies. They are real men and women whom I know: professional people, trading people, learned and ignorant, rich and poor. . . . In all my preparation it keeps me in touch with real men and women, moving in the common streets, exposed to life's varying weathers, the 'garish day' and the cold night, the gentle dew and the driving blast. It keeps me on the common earth: It saves me from losing myself in the clouds."[5]

Harry Emerson Fosdick was a great preacher of a generation ago. Nobody could preach like Fosdick. Even his critics and enemies, who were many, admitted that. He gave long and meticulous care to preparing each sermon, and each was a beautifully created and highly-polished piece of homiletical artistry. His manuscript was completed by Friday afternoon. The next stage, which was the most important of all, came on Saturday morning when he went over his sermon with his congregation before him in his mind's eye. He didn't want his pride or love of rhetoric to get between his sermon and his people. In the morning at 11 o'clock, there would be a family still in grief, having lost the father just a month ago; a woman recovering from a nervous breakdown; a young business executive about to break under the pressures of a big corporation; a young person, brilliant and gifted, but living beneath his best possibilities; a black man wondering if the church really wanted him; and many others who were in great need of some word of hope. Often this meant the excision of favorite words and phrases, even paragraphs. This was sometimes painful, but he wanted to make sure that the word he preached reached the people. And it usually did.

John D. Rockefeller, Jr., a faithful member of Riverside Church, New York City, where Fosdick was pastor, is reported to have said about his pastor's preaching: "The greatness of his preaching lies in the fact that each person in the congregation thinks he is preaching to him. I never hear him but I say, 'How does he know my problem?'" If Rockefeller had been aware of the meticulous care with which Fosdick related the message of his sermon to the people who would be before him on Sunday morning, he would likely have been in a better position to answer his question.

George Buttrick once wrote of the difference between a sermon and an essay: The sermon is written "with the eyes of the congregation (wistful, hungry, sad, or gayly indifferent) looking at the writer over his desk."[6] The essay is much more impersonal and abstract.

Buttrick once told of a discipline he practiced when he was pastor of the Madison Avenue Presbyterian Church in New York City. On Saturday night he went to the sanctuary of the church and walked its aisles. As he did, he felt he could almost slap the shoulders of people who would be sitting in those pews within a few hours. It was a reminder that he would be preaching, not to abstractions, but to real human beings who would bring all kinds of pain, doubt, frustration, and desperation, hoping to hear some healing word.

Donald Macleod, professor of homiletics at Princeton Theological Seminary, tells about some tourists at a lookout point on Mount Tom in New England. In the group was a little old lady in her seventies who lived in a clapboard house at the base of the mountain. The guide was pointing to the sweeping, panoramic beauty of the scenery before them—descending slopes, hills, valleys, and a winding river. In the midst of the excitement, the little woman pointed to her modest house and, without being self-conscious at all, exclaimed: "There is where I live!" Macleod says we should always find that point in our sermon.

When we have been faithful in bringing the text and faces together in preparation, we may be reasonably sure of the results: the text will reach people where they are struggling and living, and it may well be the most important word they will hear all week.

Robert McAfee Brown, reflecting on the living and personal quality of the Bible, has said: "The Bible is a special delivery letter with your name and address on it."[7]

What preacher has not validated the truth of which Brown speaks? In dealing with some vital biblical theme from the pulpit, God's Word becomes very personal. Often the people in the congregation feel as if God is paging them, calling them by name, and saying, "I have good news for you!" When that happens, as it often does, we experience how wonderful preaching can be, and we know that we could never be happy doing anything else.

I remember a young man, whom I had known all his life, saying to me at the close of a morning worship service: "When you were about one third through your sermon, I felt that your message was for me. It was as if I were in the sanctuary alone and you were talking to me."

A small boy was taken by his mother to the Metropolitan Tabernacle in London to hear Charles Haddon Spurgeon preach. The sermon was still in its opening stage when the boy tugged at his mother's arm and said, "Mother, is Mr. Spurgeon talking to me?"

Another story is told about a mother and her little daughter hearing Spurgeon preach. He seemed to be speaking so directly to their home life that the child whispered to her mother, "Mother, how does Mr. Spurgeon know so much about our family?"

It will help us to remember that the word of God should be preached to people on two levels of life—the permanent and the temporary.[8]

Men and women have a permanent stance. We will always find them standing there, it matters not what age, place, or culture. It doesn't matter what race, class, or nationality. There is that deep level where men and women always meet. It is on that level where they weep and laugh, work and play, despair and hope; where they are lonely, yet seek fellowship; where they are alienated, but want friends; where they are separated, yet want to be united; where they are in bondage, yet want freedom; anxious, yet seek peace; broken, yet want to be whole; where they are greedy, but generous; kind, but cruel; pray while being profane; where they love and hate; believe and doubt; seek God, yet flee from him; and they are always sinful and mortal. Men and women everywhere are shadowed by their guilt and cannot escape the night of their death. They want forgiveness and they want life.

When you recognize the permanent stance, you don't have to work so hard in making the gospel relevant. It has a built-in relevance. The word of God on its way to us has passed through this permanent stance and knows where people always stand. When we have released the word, it knows how to find its way back to those deep levels of life.

Then there is the temporary stance. These people stand in the shifting scenes of their world, in the time and place peculiar to them. No one has ever stood there before and no one will ever stand exactly there again. Each generation has moods that will pass with them. They ask some questions that have not been asked and will not be asked again.

Think, for example of how many of our serious problems are new to us. The generations before us did not have to face them. Take for example, the possibility of nuclear war, the shortage of gas and oil, the environmental crisis in its acute form, and the threat of overpopulation. The space age is new to us. Think of the new ethical problems presented by our technology such as heart transplants, test tube babies, and the radical altering of life through genetic control. While world hunger has always been a problem, we are much more aware of it than any generation before us and have a stronger sense of responsibility to do something about it. Its tragedy is brought into our living rooms on our television screens.

It is important to address the temporary stance. The problems are very serious and will not easily go away. In speaking to them our people will know that we are in touch with our world and that we care, and it may open doors to life on its deeper and more permanent level.

As we preach, we should know that the gospel we preach will long outlast the news of today, and is more relevant than the headlines of the morning newspaper. Let us take hope. Preaching can be in touch with life.

10
God's Word in
Our Words

There could be no preaching unless God had spoken. It is the Word of God that not only makes preaching possible but that makes it unique, saving it from being just another discourse. David H. C. Read has defined preaching as the encounter "of modern man with the Word of God." It is the Word of God that has created the pulpit and it is the Word of God that sustains it.

What if God had spoken, yet in a language that is strange, esoteric, and noncommunicable? What if his language were so mysterious that it eluded us completely? What if it were a kind of code the keys of which we do not have? Preaching still couldn't happen. The Word of God has to be hearable and communicable. It is only as the Word of God can be translated into human speech that preaching is possible, and fortunately that can happen. The Word of God comes to us with a human accent.

GOD'S WORD

We can stand most things better than silence, and few things are more destructive. Simple people, who do not understand the dynamic of silence, will sometimes pick it up intuitively as a cudgel with which to destroy those whom they should love and be close to. The refusal to communicate with a person dehumanizes him, turning him into a thing. That can destroy his sense of worth and personhood. I remember one of the unhappiest people I have known telling how her family was destroyed. "Silence was my weapon," she said.

One of the cruelest kinds of torture is solitary confinement. Isolate a person so he cannot see a face, nor hear a voice or footfall, and he will be pushed to the brink of insanity. Some of our soldiers during the Vietnam War underwent this kind of treatment when they were prisoners. They have told us of its maddening effects.

Who has not been frightened by the silence of the heavens? We feel so small beneath their vastness and we feel so lonely. We would like to speak to them, but we know they cannot hear or answer us. There is a silence even more frightening than that of the stars. That is the silence of God.

What if the heart of the universe were as speechless as the stars? What if, when we talked to God, we heard only the echo of our voices? What if complete silence hung over the great questions about life? What if no light pierced the darkness and mystery of life? What if no voice came from beyond us to tell us who we are, where we came from, and where we are going? Our planet would be a madhouse. We sometimes feel it is that already, but it would be infinitely worse if no voice had broken the silence.

Basic to our faith is the claim that God has spoken, that he has broken the terrible silence of life. Indeed, he has said the decisive word without which life doesn't make sense and without which we cannot live.

It is true that we have never seen God nor heard him speak audibly. What then is this Word of God? It can be such a baffling, confusing, and mysterious term. What does the Bible mean when it speaks of the Word of God? It is important that we know since we have been called to speak it. If it is elusive to us who speak from the pulpit, it will certainly be elusive to those who hear in the pews.

What then is this Word of God? It is God creating. He

created by the power of his word. He spoke and creation happened. A refrain, "and God said," runs through the creation story in the first chapter of Genesis. It is God communicating his truth to his prophets, servants, ministers, and people. The Word of God is God present with us, loving us, and caring for us. It is God meeting us, encountering us, and addressing us. It is God judging us, rebuking us, and wounding us on the jagged and cutting edges of his moral law. It is God binding up our wounds in mercy and healing us in grace. It is God with us, suffering for us, getting beneath the terrible burden of our guilt and shame. It is God in commonplace and in the not so commonplace events that are sometimes shattering and mystifying. It is God supremely acting in the birth, life, death, and resurrection of Jesus Christ. Nowhere else is his word so powerful and his accent so clear. Nowhere is God so articulate in a saving way as in the cross and empty tomb of Jesus Christ. That is why these two events form the center of the Christian gospel. It is true that the cross and empty tomb do not solve the riddle of sin and death but they do a better thing—they point to the power by which the two are overcome.

It must be said that communication is difficult. Indeed, one of our basic human problems is the failure of communication. How often we say one thing and people hear us saying something else. Communication fails on all levels of life. It happens in the home where we know one another the best, and where communication should be clearest and most easily understood. How often the child doesn't understand what his parents are saying, and how often the language and ideas of the child seem strange to the parents. Communication fails along the streets where people meet, in places of business, in clubs and fraternities, in classrooms and in pulpits. Communication is particularly difficult when it takes place across class, cultural, religious, racial, and national lines. Language seems especially garbled there.

I think of how my sermons have been reported across the years, not in a malicious way but sometimes inaccurately. Obviously, I was saying one thing while some in my congregation were hearing me saying something else.

If we human beings have difficulty in making each other understand what we are saying, what an enormous problem God must have in making us understand what he is saying to us. Has not God said: "For as the heavens are higher than the earth,/so are my ways higher than your ways/and my thoughts than your thoughts?" (Isa. 55:9). How can a God who walks in mystery and whose thoughts are high above ours ever make us understand what he is saying to us? That is an extremely important question.

Our faith, of course, affirms that God can speak to us in ways we can understand. If he can't, then our religion is robbed of one of its basic affirmations. It becomes too subjective. We can't be sure our faith is anything more than a projection of our wishful thinking. Our religion is the way we wish things were but we cannot be sure that they are that way at all. We cannot be certain that our religious ideas have any corresponding objective reality.

Let me suggest that God finds communication with us possible for three reasons: He is speaking to a world he has made, we can be hearers and communicators of that word because we have been made in the image of God, and history is accessible to God as the sphere of revelation and saving action.

God has created our world and the marks of his creatorship are on it. It is very much like seeing a beautiful house and being able to say: "I know the architect. He has built himself into that house." Or it is like seeing an elegant piece of furniture and being able to say: "I know the craftsman. His marks are unmistakable on it." God's marks are unmistakable on his world. Therefore, the psalmist could say: "The heavens are telling the glory of God;/and the firmament proclaims his handiwork" (Ps.

19:1). "Ever since the creation of the world," Paul said, "his invisible nature, namely, his eternal power and deity, has been clearly perceived in the things that have been made" (Rom. 1:20).

Jesus could take a grain of wheat and hear God's voice in it. One of God's basic principles of the universe, namely that sacrifice can issue in life, was written into that little seed. Hear Jesus: "Truly, truly, I say to you, unless a grain of wheat fall into the earth and dies, it remains alone; but if it dies, it bears much fruit. He who loves his life loses it, and he who hates his life in the world will keep it for eternal life" (John 12:24-25).

When Jesus instituted the Lord's Supper, he took a piece of bread which had come originally from the wheat fields and wine which had come from the vineyards and made them the vehicles of the great truths he wanted to pass on through this memorial. He could use simple things from God's natural creation to communicate great truths from God.

There is a basic sense in which we can speak of the universe as being sacramental. Nature can be the bearer of God's presence, his grace, and his word.

Again, it is possible for God to speak to us because we are made in the image of God. Here God has a point of contact when speaking to us. It is true that that image has been blurred, almost completely defaced in some cases. Yet, we can, even the most injured of us, hear at least the faint trace of God's voice.

We can be like the boy Samuel, to whom God spoke. We can so easily mistake God's voice for other voices. We think others are calling when in reality it may be God speaking to us. Samuel thought it was the old priest, Eli, calling him. When he learned of his mistake, he said, "Speak, for thy servant hears" (1 Sam. 3:10). Just so with us. We can say: "Speak, Lord, I am a hearer."

God can also speak to us because history is open to his saving deeds. He, of course, is above the flex, change, and flow of history. Because he is, a thousand years in his sight are but as yesterday when it is past or as a watch in the night. There is a real sense in which God does not see time as we do. He is above it and observes it from a vantage point from which we can never look at it. But there is a sense in which God can see history and experiences time the way we do since he acts in history. He can know, as we do, the pain and anguish of the years. He is in them, and it is here, in our history, where we hear most clearly his word and see most distinctly, his saving deeds. We can speak of Christianity as being a historical religion since history is the essential sphere of God's revelation and redeeming action. God can know the burden and fatigue of our dusty ways since he in his Son has walked in them.

Since our world is the kind of world with which God can communicate, let us ask more specifically: How does he communicate? Let me suggest four ways: through personal encounter, historical events, persons, and supremely through one person, Jesus of Nazareth.

It becomes obvious from biblical faith that God addresses people personally. I have just mentioned the boy Samuel. Could Moses ever forget his experience before the burning bush on the backside of a desert when God addressed him, "Moses, Moses?" (Ex. 3:4). Paul could never escape his encounter with the living Lord when he was addressed: "Saul, Saul, why do you persecute me?" (Acts 9:4). It is extremely interesting to note in the Bible how often a person becomes aware of who he is, what he is to do, or have his life launched in a radically new direction becaue he is personally addressed by God.

We are addressed by so many people under so many conditions, and they all have significance. It is no little thing to hear one's name called. Yet, we forget so many of these even though they were very important to us at the time. But who can forget the day, likely a time of crisis, when God spoke to you, offering forgiveness, giving hope, strengthening your self-image, or clarifying vocational choice? How could we forget it? It was the turning point in our lives.

God also speaks to us in historical events. Ours is an event-oriented religion. We hang our faith on events. Who can forget Abraham and his caravan moving westward, leaving a trail of dust across the desert, not knowing where he was going but knowing that God had called him to go somewhere? Who can forget Jacob's meeting God in the wilderness, which was a most unlikely place to meet God? Who can forget the bondage in Egypt, the Exodus to freedom at the Red Sea, the giving of the law at Mount Sinai, and the enacting of the covenant? Who can forget the captivity in faraway Babylon where they could not sing the Lord's song in a strange land, the release from that captivity, and a remnant returning home with shouts of joy on their lips? Who can forget Bethlehem, Calvary, and the garden tomb? Who can forget the Holy Spirit mightily empowering the church on the Day of Pentecost? Who can forget Saul of Tarsus's shattering experience along the Damascus road? Who can forget the first church being established on Gentile soil in Antioch of Syria? Who can forget the mighty missionary movement, like a great stream washing a sinful and polluted world, that went forth from that church?

God's Word has not been given to us as if we were stenographers taking dictation, certainly not as if we were passive tapes on which God recorded his message. No, God spoke through living history, through events, and the Holy Spirit, like a shaft of light, pierced the shadowed and darkened landscape of history so we could see what God was doing.

God has further spoken to us through historical persons, especially through prophets, who gave a fresh word from God, essentially to their time and place. I am thinking in particular of the great eighth-century prophets, who spoke both a word of judgment and hope. They knew God's judgment was fierce, that his wrath was like a consuming fire. But the God who cut and wounded also healed, the God who spoke of darkness also spoke of light, and the God who uttered words of devastation also offered words of hope. While the word of the prophet was, as has already been said, a word for his time, there was a timelessness about what he said. He spoke for all times. Take, for example, the words of Micah: "He has showed you, O man, what is good;/and what does the Lord require of you/but to do justice and to love kindness/and to walk humbly with your God?" (Mic. 6:8). We don't have to argue with Micah. We know that is the Word of God. There is something about it that makes it self-authenticating, and you realize it is as much for our time as it was for his. God is still speaking through Micah, and what a compelling word it is.

Finally, as earlier mentioned, God has spoken his word in greatest finality and clearest accent in Jesus of Nazareth. The author of Hebrews who said that God had spoken by the prophets went on to say "but in these last days has spoken to us by a Son, whom he appointed the heir of all things, through whom also he created the world" (Heb. 1:2).

It was in Jesus of Nazareth that God's Word took on its most human accent and greatest authority. Jesus Christ was truly human as he was truly divine.

We remember Jesus' saying to his disciples: "He who has seen me has seen the Father" (John 14:9). It was such a radical thing to say. Yet, it has become so commonplace that we lose the wonder of it. We are no longer startled by it, we speak it so glibly. The words have been worn smooth by common usage. But imagine the original shock his disciples must have experienced. There Jesus stood before them, a carpenter from Nazareth, his face tanned by the sun, his hands calloused by carpenter's tools. Sweat rolled down his face as he worked in his father's carpenter shop in Nazareth on a hot summer day, and he probably knew what it was to stand in wood shavings ankle deep. He was so human, and although he said this extremely radical thing about himself they could not have missed the human accent.

God accommodated himself to us little people in Jesus Christ. In the incarnation, God took upon himself our frail and fragile form. God was like a father who gets down on the floor with his three-year-old son on Christmas morning. He doesn't tower above his son, but seeks to make himself little the way the child is. He thinks the thoughts of a child and uses the language of a child. He makes sure his little boy can understand him. Rather than trying to lift his son to his level, he gets down on the level of the son. He accommodates himself to the child. Yet, while using simple language, they talk about very profound things—surprise, wonder, mystery, love, giving, joy, and laughter. God has done that in Jesus Christ, yet in a much more wonderful way. We can understand him. He does indeed have a human accent.

While I have indicated that the world God made is a point of communication for him, and while nature tells us something about God, I have not been able to say that nature is one of the basic ways in which God speaks his word to us. It is not, and the Bible never claims that it is. Therefore, nature must be omitted as a basic way through which God communicates with us and that for two reasons. First, the word we get through nature is often ambiguous and the language of nature is often slurred speech. Nature is not only kind and generous; nature is often heartless and ruthless. Nature not only gives spring showers and balmy days; nature sends droughts and tornados. It is often difficult to see a loving and provident God in nature. The word we get from her is often not clear.

Second, while a bridge which an engineer has designed can tell you much about his knowledge and skill, it cannot tell you about his character and values. The bridge cannot let you know whether he is faithful to his wife, loves his children, is a good neighbor, or is a man of honor and integrity. Just so with nature. It cannot tell us about the mind and heart of God, and that is really what we want to know. This we have seen supremely in Jesus.

IN OUR WORDS

God's Word is like his salvation. He doesn't save us out of our world but in it, nor does he save us outside history but in it. God doesn't remove us from our common setting into some ethereal realm and there address us. While his word comes from beyond us, he speaks to us along our common and mundane ways. Since God speaks to us where we are, and because his word has come to us in personal address, historical events, historical persons, and supremely in Jesus of Nazareth, we can understand it. Because God's Word has a human accent, we can put his word into our words.

When the Word of God finds expression in our words, there is a real sense in which incarnation takes place. The Word of God again becomes flesh.

David H. C. Read says that preaching is "the word made flesh in contemporary language. It is a vehicle of the Spirit whereby the real presence of Christ is realized. . . . I make no apology for talking about practical matters of style, method, and technique. For what we are considering is the expression of the Word of God in the language of today. Expression here means incarnation—the Word of God taking on the flesh of our daily speech."[1]

Clyde Fant has a theory of preaching which he calls incarnational. "Theology itself provides us with the decisive clue," he writes. "The divine-human nature of its concern are precisely those of preaching: 'The Word became flesh and dwelt among us' (John 1:14, RSV). Form, methodology, and delivery are nothing more, and nothing less, than the Word of God taking on flesh and dwelling among us. . . . The incarnation, therefore, is the truest theological model for preaching because it was

God's ultimate act of communication. Jesus, who was the Christ, most perfectly said God to us because the eternal work took on human flesh in a contemporary situation. Preaching cannot do otherwise."[2]

There are many illustrations of how the Word of God can be clothed in our human words. Let us, for example, see how the Word of God can be spoken in our relational language.

Relationships are the very essence of life. Broken relationships can tell of the tragedy of life, while the healing of basic relationships can tell of our salvation. We have both bad news and good news from God. The bad news is that basic relationships have been broken. We are separated and cut off from the sources and springs of life. The good news is that God has taken the kind of action that makes possible the healing of these broken relationships.

We can speak of broken relationships in our four basic environments—natural, personal, social, and spiritual. Here is life's tragedy, but the good news is that these broken relationships can be healed.

Nature forms our natural environment. Nature is our home. She cradles us. She is the stage where we play out our human drama, where our history unfolds, where we make our human pilgrimage. We speak of the good earth, as indeed we should. She has given us birth, nurtures us, and sustains us.

We should recognize our kinship to nature. When I sift rich loamy soil through my fingers, drink from a spring of fresh water, feel the cool grass beneath my bare feet, experience a gentle breeze blowing on my face on a hot sultry day, I know that nature is not alien to me. I know I am kin to nature and that nature is kin to me.

St. Francis in his *Canticle to the Sun* recognizes our kinship to nature. He speaks of Brother Sun, Sister Moon, Brother Wind, Sister Water, and Mother Earth.

Yet, we do not always properly regard nature. She becomes an object which we manipulate and exploit, turning her into easy profit. All too often the dollar mark, like a shadow, lies across our most beautiful landscapes. We have been irresponsible, wasteful, and prodigal with nature. We have given little thought to those who will come after us. Earth will be their home, as it has been ours. We should leave them a beautiful, clean, and fruitful place.

We are often alienated from nature. Our relationship with her is a broken one. We need to be reconciled with her, to have our broken relationships healed. Our gospel is comprehensive enough to be concerned about this kind of reconciliation. Not even the most mundane realities of life escape the attention of our gospel. Christ can heal this brokenness, and help us to establish a loving, caring, and protective relationship with nature.

When St. Francis met Christ, even his vision of the physical world was different. He said the sky was bluer, the flowers were brighter, and the bird sang more sweetly. The whole earth seemed to be bathed in a fresh, new light.

There is a break in the inner self which is my personal environment. There is a war going on inside me. Two selves seem to be locked in mortal combat. I am separated from my better self, that self I was meant to be and want to be in my best moments. Alas, the bad, alien self seems often to get the upper hand.

George Buttrick once said: "I have a cleft will and the cleft is down the center." That is the kind of will each of us has, and no one knew it better than Paul. "I do not understand my own actions," he wrote. "For I do not do what I want, but I do the very thing I hate" (Rom. 7:15). Who does not know what Paul was talking about?

I remember my son, as a small boy, doing something that was very offensive to me. Angrily I asked: "Chip, why did you do it?" No answer. With greater intensity I asked the second time. Still no answer. I put the question very strongly the third time. Then he gave a most disarming answer: "I don't know why I did it." And his daddy remembered those many times when he could not explain his own behavior. I have so often suffered defeat in the inner struggle.

How do you heal the cleft will, resolve the inner conflict, and mend the broken inner relationship? The answer is basically a religious one. Paul in a desperate moment, when he was about to go down in defeat, came upon victory. He cried out: "Who will deliver me?" Then the exclamation of victory: "Thanks be to God through Jesus Christ our Lord!" (Rom. 7:25). God had acted in such a way in Christ that the broken relationship within himself could be healed, victory could be his.

Lloyd C. Douglas in a sermon, "The Mirror," has Jesus to ask Zacchaeus, the tax collector, "Zacchaeus, what did you see that made you desire this peace?" "Good master," came the reply, "I saw mirrored in your eyes the face of the Zacchaeus I was meant to be." It is that self I was meant to be that is so elusive, and only Christ can enable me to become that self.

There is a break in my relationship with my brother which is my social environment.

That is a terrible break. It is very painful and sometimes destructive. I need the brother. I need hands that reach out and touch me, voices that call me by name, feet that strike cadence and walk with me, and persons who will accept me and declare my worth. I need people who will love me and whom I can love, people who will serve me and allow me to serve them. I am incurably social. I need community.

Who can heal the broken relationship between my brother and me? Who can make me feel close to those who seem so far away? Who can tear down those high barriers that divide us? Who can turn my hate for the brother into love for him? Who can enable me to forgive and accept forgiveness? Christ can.

We cannot forget the church. It is the family of Christ, the community of faith. I know how weak, false, and hypocritical the church can be, how far short it falls of Christ's expectation of it. And, yet, despite its weakness, I am glad to say this about the church: I have seen more loving people and more love in it than anywhere else. The church helps me fulfill my need for the brother.

I am thinking of a boy who was painfully isolated and cut off from people. He would not talk. Then the members of a church showed love to that boy and reached out to him. They, in many ways, affirmed him and declared his worth. He began to talk, becoming very articulate. I saw a church love that boy into speech and articulation. That was enough miracle for me.

Finally, there is a break in my relationship with God which is my spiritual environment.

As already indicated, this is the primal break. Because of this we suffer broken relationships in the other basic environments of our life. If I were right with God, I would love the other person who is God's child and therefore my brother or sister. I would see worth and dignity in every life regardless of nationality, race, or class. There would be no barrier too high for me to reach across and touch another life.

If my broken relationship with God had been healed, I would be healed on the inside because my life would be centered in God. It would not be caught in cross-purposes because I would love God with all the powers of my life. I would have a strong center around which all my loyalties would gather in service to one overarching purpose.

If my life were right with God, I would see nature as God's creation which he has entrusted to human hands for keeping. I would not want to wound and bleed her, nor exploit her for selfish gain. I would want to increase her beauty, make her more productive, enhance her wealth, and pass her unspoiled to those who will come after me.

The good news of the gospel is concerned with this primal

break. Here is the heart of our gospel: God in Christ makes it possible for our broken relationship with him to be healed. He has overcome our estrangement, overridden our separation, and drawn us to himself in peace. And the wonder of it all is that it is of grace. Forgiveness is free, salvation is a gift. Paul could speak of God's salvation as a "free gift."

One of the best friends I ever had was an arrested alcoholic. I knew him in his bad years when he had "hit bottom." He had already lost self-esteem, and was losing everything of value. After he had received help, he wanted to share it. I often called him about a person in the throes of alcoholism. The night was never too cold nor the day too hot for him to go to the distressed person. He once told me a story about his last visit to a hospital to be "dried out." While there he was befriended by a little nurse. One day she said to him: "I want you to hear a man from Alcoholics Anonymous speak tonight. (It was in the early days of that fine movement). My friend said he had other plans for the evening, but he could not refuse the invitation from his dear friend. At 7:30 he was at the meeting. The speaker was a man in his middle thirties who had gone to the pinnacle of success and then, because of alcoholism, had fallen precipitously to the bottom. He was now a sober man and was on the way up again. My friend said he had never heard such a story. When the speaker came to the close of his message, he asked: "Is there one of you fellows who would like to be sober again?" My friend said his arm shot up, he could not keep it down. "Yes," he said, "I would like to be sober again. I would give every cent I've got to be a sober man again." And the speaker said to him: "You can be a sober man again and it won't cost you a cent."

That is what God says to us. When we come to him wanting our broken relationship healed: "You can be healed and it won't cost you a cent. My healing is of grace. It is a gift."

We who preach need to hope again in the power of the spoken word. We are sometimes intimidated by a visual culture.

We are bombarded by visual imagery on all sides, but, contrary to popular belief, the Word is more powerful than the picture. It speaks to deep primordial levels that the picture cannot touch.

We should remember the faith the religion of Israel put in the power of words. Her sanctuaries were empty of pictures and statuary of all kinds. But Israel knew there was power in the spoken word, and her prophets knew it, too. We should not forget that Jesus was a spokesman, not a penman or an artist.

How exciting preaching would be if we could believe that God's Word can be spoken in our words. This we can believe!

11
Two Vital Questions: What Then? What Now?

The authentic preacher cannot escape tension. He cannot be too relaxed. He must stand with one foot in the biblical world and the other in the modern world. With one hand he holds on tenaciously to the past, while the other one is laid sensitively on the present moment.

The biblical message comes out of the past, a long past. The message of the pulpit is concerned with the saving events of God that took place in history. It is concerned with one above all others—the Christ event. Yet, that past is not dead; it lives. That powerful influence carries over into the present and can be one of those tremendous forces that molds, shapes, and directs us into the future. The preacher has to go back into the biblical past and ask, what then? Unless he asks that question honestly and searchingly, he cannot speak with authority.

The preacher also has to feel the tremors of modern life and hear the tumultuous voices that cry out. He has to ask, what now? Unless he asks that question sensitively and perceptively, he cannot contemporize the biblical message. He cannot be relevant.

Often the tragedy of preaching is that we ask only one of these questions, or place disproportionate emphasis on one while neglecting the other.

I have always been tempted to leave Jesus on his donkey

along a wayside in first-century Palestine. It is a safe place. If I bring him into the city he may stir up the people. He had a way of doing that. Yet, I can't really be authentic and relevant unless I leave him along city streets or by roads humming with modern motors. However, there is no use to bring him into the city unless I have seen him on his donkey along an ancient wayside. Unless I see him there, I can't really understand who he is. Why introduce Jesus Christ to a modern congregation unless we know who he is?

We have to ask these two questions about the text we are to preach on next Sunday. But before we ask these, we have to select the Scripture and text.

CHOOSING THE TEXT

This will be a hard job unless we know our Bibles. Therefore, back of choosing a text should be consistent, systematic Bible study in depth. A preacher should know its great themes that occur over and over again like the theme of a symphony.

The preacher should be not only a student of the Bible but of the world as well. He should know the dynamics, values, moods, questions, conflicts, the despair, and the hope of the world. He should be clued into his generation.

Then when he comes to choose his text, with one eye on the biblical theme and the other on faces he meets along the streets of his town and sees in his congregation, he will make a wonderful discovery: Texts will often leap out at him, asking to be preached. Often it will not be so much his seeking texts, as texts seeking him, and when they find him they may lay imperious hands on him, demanding to be preached. Here lies one of the exciting realities about preaching.

Fosdick once spoke of the wonder of this kind of thing. "Any preacher who, with even moderate skill, is there helping folk to solve their real problems is functioning. . . . This did not mean that the Bible's importance in preaching diminished. Upon the contrary, I have been suckled on the Bible, knew it, and loved it, and I could not deal with any crucial problem in thought and life without seeing text after text lift its hands begging to be used. The Bible came alive to me."[1]

I like the metaphor—text after text lifting up its hands begging to be preached. You can't know how wonderful that is until it has happened to you.

David H. C. Read has written of this kind of thing: "There are occasions—in my experience comparatively rare—when a text or a topic grabs one by the throat, you know that this is what must be preached next Sunday. Normally, I find that the decision comes from wrestling with the two factors that control the preacher's task—the Scriptures and the *kairos. Kairos* is the Greek word which the New Testament writers employed to indicate time as actual and decisive (for clock time, a linear succession of events, they used the word *chronos*). *Kairos* is the existential moment, and I am using it here to indicate the preacher's sense of what is happening in the world, in the community, in the church, in the congregation, right now. Without the Scripture the preacher will have nothing to say to *kairos*, except to analyze, to criticize, or to offer some hints as to how we can struggle along with a certain amount of success and peace of mind. Without the *kairos* the preacher will find himself declaring biblical truths that seem to hang in the air without any attachment to life as his hearers are experiencing.

"In my experience the first thought of the sermon comes either from the passage of Scripture that seems to speak to the *kairos*, or from some pressure of the *kairos* that suggests a search in the Scriptures."[2]

Once the text has been selected, it is well to read it in the original language if you have that kind of skill. Only as one is able to read the text in the original language is one fully able to feel the peculiar flavor and quality of the truth, see its subtle imagery, and discover its delicate shades of meaning.

When we cannot use the original language, fortunately we have available several reliable translations. We should use these. Even the preacher who can read from the original will find that these translations have value. The labor and fruit of these linguistic scholars will be helpful to him or her.

Let us see how reading the text from several translations can be helpful. Take for example, Romans 5:20*b*. Note various translations of that wonderful text. King James Version: "Where sin abounded, grace did much more abound." Revised Standard Version: "Where sin increased, grace abounded all the more." *The New English Bible*: "Where sin was thus multiplied, grace immeasurably exceeded it." The *Good News Bible*: "Where sin increased, God's grace increased much more." *The Jerusalem Bible*: "But however great the number of sins committed, grace was even greater." *The New Testament in Modern English* (J. B. Phillips): "Though sin is shown to be wide and deep, thank God his grace is wider and deeper still!"

We see immediately how these translations open up new vistas of possibilities for the text. While all translations are faithful to the basic truth, there are nuances of thought, variations in shades of meaning, and fresh imagery. Take, for example, Phillips's translation. Note the imagery which is concrete and vivid. The truth becomes more alive if the imagery is fresh and picturesque. This makes one want to preach the text.

Or take another great text: 2 Corinthians 5:19*a*. Observe various translations of it. King James Version: "God was in Christ, reconciling the world unto himself, not imputing their trespasses unto them." Revised Standard Version: "In Christ God was reconciling the world to himself, not counting their trespasses against them." *The New English Bible*: "God was in Christ, reconciling the world to himself, no longer holding men's misdeeds against them." The *Good News Bible*: "Our message is that God was making all mankind his friends through Christ. God did not keep account of their sins." *The Jerusalem Bible*: "God was in Christ reconciling the world to himself, not holding men's faults against them." *The New Testament in Modern English* (J. B. Phillips): "God was in Christ personally reconciling the world to himself—not counting their sins against them."

The same thing can be said of the translations of this text as was said of the first. There are nuances of thought, changing shades of delicate meaning, and imagery that grips one's mind. I would like to preach this text, combining the translations by The *Good News Bible* and Phillips. When combined, the truth is very warm, intimate, and personal. The *Good News Bible* says God was making friends of us while Phillips's translation tells us that God was doing it personally.

I think the advantage of using several translations in interpreting the text is obvious.

WHAT THEN?

In answering this important question, I think the preacher should do two things. First, seek to understand the original meaning of the passage and text. Here is where the basic exegetical work is done for a sermon. Second, after having done the basic exegetical work, seek to enter the historical situation imaginatively and reenter the situation. In some real sense be there. Identify with the people in the far-off time and place. Seek to see with their eyes, hear with their ears, touch with their hands, and feel with their hearts. Sense their strength and weakness, their courage and cowardice. Laugh with them and weep with them. Hope with them and despair with them.

Nothing has the power to bring ancient truth to life as does the imagination. Situations which seem to be nothing more than dead experiences from the past will come alive. People who are as dead as mummies will live again. Voices long silenced will speak again. One's imagination, of course, should not be allowed to run wild. It must be used responsibly, which is made possible by keeping it in touch with reality. Bring to life only those things that did happen or could have happened. Do not indulge your imagination in the fanciful and unreal. That is very dangerous indeed.

I have spoken about texts that leap out at one, demanding to be preached. There is nothing more exciting but it is not without its dangers. The experience can be too subjective. It can allow the text to touch unduly some emotionally sensitive spot, support some pet idea, or strengthen some bias. Therefore, I need to test the experience by an objective reality and nothing is better than solid bibilical scholarship. Such scholarship can be the touchstone by which I test the validity of the experience. I should have at hand a good commentary, a biblical dictionary, a theological wordbook, and other tools.

Six questions will be helpful as you do your exegetical work.

First, the basic exegetical question: What is the meaning of the text? In answering that question, read out the meaning of the text, and explicate its truth. Do not read into it some pet idea. Let the text say what it wants to say, not what you wish it would say.

Give careful attention to the meaning of words, particularly key words and how they are related in phrases and sentences.

Let us assume that the text will be Ephesians 2:8-9: "For by grace you have been saved through faith; and this is not your own doing, it is the gift of God—not because of works, lest any man should boast."

The two key words in the text are *grace* and *faith*. What does *grace* mean? It can mean favor, gracious care, goodwill. Its basic meaning is unmerited love. It means gift which we could never earn or be worthy of. Grace is the essential way in which God has acted in Christ.

What is the meaning of faith? To have faith means to trust,

to repose, to rely on, to place myself upon, to commit my life. I do not come to God bearing gifts nor displaying my moral virtues. I come with empty hands. I have nothing to bring except my own emptiness and brokenness. But that is enough. I trust the grace of God the way a drowning man does a life raft that is shoved to him. He gets on it, relies completely upon it, and is saved from the threatening sea. I trust the grace of God in Christ completely, I accept salvation as a gift. I can never boast nor feel proud. There is nothing I did for my salvation. Salvation is something that was done for me. It is of grace.

Grace is the objective side of salvation, the divine side. God has acted graciously for us in Jesus Christ. Faith is the subjective side of salvation, the human side. We accept that which has been done so graciously for us.

Second, the historical question: What happened then and there?

As has been suggested several times, Christianity is a historical religion. Our faith has not come to us mystically, nor through intellectual speculation, nor through flashes of intuitive insight, nor through universal truth held in the human mind. God has disclosed himself through deeds, events, and persons in history. There are dates, places, faces, and names written across our faith. We ask such simple questions as who, when, where, how, and why?

You may be preaching on that magnificent Scripture, the fortieth chapter of Isaiah, where the eternal, transcendent God is contrasted with the people who are completely dispirited and exhausted. Why are the people so weary? Why do the hearts of youth fail and why are young men utterly worn out? We can't answer those questions unless we understand the historical background. The author is writing in a concentration camp in ancient Babylon. The people are away from home, uprooted, in an alien land with seemingly no future. How could they be any other way than depressed and depleted? Their hope lies in the transcendent God who will stoop to their need, renewing them.

   Third: The contextual question: What is the setting of the text?

   The preacher has to understand the text within context, what goes before it and what comes after it. Never lift a word from the sentence of which it is a part, nor a verse from its chapter, nor a chapter from its book. And never lift a book from the context of the entire Bible. So many false movements have gotten started, so many heresies have come about, so many splinter groups have been formed, because a word, a verse, a chapter, or a book has been lifted out of context.

   If we are to understand a tropical flower, we have to study it in its tropical setting. If we isolate it from its environment, as, for example, transposing it to the Arctic, we can't understand it. Just so with a text. It has to be interpreted in context.

   Suppose we are preaching from the ninth chapter of Romans and take as our text, "So then he has mercy upon whomever he wills, and he hardens the heart of whomever he wills" (Rom. 9:18); or, "Has the potter no right over the clay, to make out of the same lump one vessel for beauty and another for menial use?" (Rom. 9:21). If we treat either one of these verses in isolation, lifting the verse from a wider context, we are in trouble. We will picture God as being sovereign with absolute power, but capricious and arbitrary. We will get a rigid predestinarianism that claims God creates certain people for heaven while he creates others for hell. We get a God more immoral than the worst of human beings.

   But Paul did not intend for those statements which he wrote to remain in isolation. He set them in a wider context where God is seen essentially as a God of mercy. As he comes near to the end of the eleventh chapter of Romans he writes: "For God has consigned all men to disobedience, that he may have mercy upon all" (Rom. 11:32).

Fourth, the theological question: What is God doing?

While the Bible records history, it is not basically a book of history. It is theological in nature. Some of the world's finest literature is found in the Bible. Yet, it is not essentially literature. It is a theological book. Therefore, we look in events, deeds, and faces to see what God is doing. We study literary forms to hear what God is saying.

The first eleven chapters of Genesis give, more than any other of the world's literature, a penetrating analysis of the human situation. They create a theological background against which the rest of the Bible unfolds. God created the universe by the power of his word. Because God is creator, life has significance. He shoved all his creation toward meaning, and set the feet of men and women in paths that go somewhere. Then came man's sin and rebellion. He became alienated from God, and brother became separated from brother. Then followed God's judgment. You see that in the Flood and the debacle at the Tower of Babel. But through it all you feel the strong overtones of God's grace. You know he loves his creation and cannot give it up.

Against that background the story of the Bible is told. In this story, we can trace God's ways in happenings, encounters, and persons, it matters not how commonplace, mundane, and historical. We especially find him in Jesus Christ. Unless we can find out what God is doing, we will miss the purpose of the Bible.

Thus in a text, we try to find out what God is doing. We may be preaching, for example on the text, "There they crucified him" (Luke 23:33). Where was God when Jesus was being crucified between two thieves, on that barren hill, and what was God doing? He was there letting evil overly extend itself. He was there judging the sins of men, not particularly the crude, vulgar sins of obviously bad men. These sins expose themselves. He was there exposing and judging the socially accepta- ble sins of respectable people. He was showing how bad "good" people can be. God was there absorbing the guilt and shame of people, and he was there forgiving sins.

Fifth, the basic question: What is the central truth of the text?

A passage or text might suggest several minor, peripheral truths which may be novel and fascinating. But what is the central truth? We are often tempted to pursue minor truths, but why do it when we have so many major ones to explore?

I have always enjoyed seeing a tributary flow into the main- stream. Where the small stream hits the big one, there are produced eddies that swirl, churn, and move erratically. Those eddies are very fascinating, but no cargo is carried on them. Only the mainstream can carry cargo. In preaching it is so easy to look for truths that are like swirling eddies. They are interesting and fascinating, appealing to the imagination. But they are no more substantial than the erratic eddies. They cannot carry the weight of great truth. If we are to do boating or carry cargo, we have to stay with the mainstream. The same is true of preaching.

Let us assume again that we are preaching on the crucifix- ion. One could easily get carried away with crucifixion as the most shameful death of the ancient world, the curious crowds that looked on, how a Roman cross was made, how a body was put on the cross and taken down from it, the stoical manner in which Roman soldiers went about executing a crucifixion, and the terrible agony of that death. These can be very interesting, and should not be completely neglected since they give realism to the historical situation. But this must not be done at the expense of great themes such as man's sin, God's judgment, and the death of Jesus as a saving event.

Sixth, the question of communication: What are the obstacles to communication?

Communication of biblical truth is not always easy. These truths come from a faraway day with strange customs, strange language, and strange thought forms. Biblical truths often have a kind of bult-in communication problem. You must be sensitive to this problem, and go to great pain to communicate clearly.

Imagine that we are preaching on Paul's concept of righteousness. What image will one's congregation associate with that term? They will likely think in behavioral terms, of living by ethical principles, of acquiring moral virtues. But that is not what Paul meant essentially. He thought in relational terms. A person believed in Christ, and God declared him in a right relationship with himself. God declared him righteous because he believed. Paul called it justification by faith. Out of that relationship came a new life-style, a new way of behaving. But first of all it was relational in nature. Right living grows out of right relationships.

Having done the basic exegetical work, we enter the historical situation imaginatively. The imagination, properly used, has the rare power of touching biblical truth to life. One of the reasons biblical preaching is often so dull and boring is that the preacher is lacking in imagination. The preacher did not recreate the historical situation in a lively way, and he did not reenter the situation imaginatively. He wasn't there when it happened.

There is a Negro spiritual that asks: "Were you there when they crucified my Lord?" I had better have been there if my message is to live through me. I can be there. If I look long enough at the motley crowd I can spot my face. It was lips like mine that hurled biting sarcasms at him and spat in his face. I would certainly have been with the respectable people representing law and order. It was they who put him to death. I would have been among those who cried, "Crucify him! Crucify him!" It was hands like my hands that in mockery threw the purple robe about his shoulders and pressed the crown of thorns on his brow. It was hands like mine that drove the spikes into his hands and pierced his side with a sword. Yes, I was there. And because I was, there may be something of the realism in my preaching that was present on that fateful day so long ago.

Let me give two examples of how I may reenter the historical situation imaginatively and then transpose the truth in a lively way into the present moment.

My first sermon would have as its title, "Healing the Rift," and my text would be, "To unite all things in him, things in heaven and things on earth" (Eph. 1:10). My second sermon's title would be, "A Man Totally Saved," and my text would be, "Today salvation has come to this house, since he also is a son of Abraham" (Luke 19:9).

In my first sermon, I would step back imaginatively into that ancient world with its divisions, brokenness, and separation, its anger, hatred, and hostility. I looked everywhere and saw frightening cleavages and chasms that threatened to swallow us up. There was the division between slaves and free men. Almost half the population consisted of slaves. I felt depressed. Slavery was like a shadow that lay across that world. There was the division between men and women. I sensed the masculinity of that world. It was a man's world. Women were little more than chattel owned by their husbands. I felt the terrible tension between Jew and Gentile. How they hated each other! I saw proud Greeks looking condescendingly on common people and sneeringly calling them barbarians. I saw pious Jews who hissed when they called Gentiles dogs.

I visited Saul in Tarsus, and I saw there the lostness of the Gentile world. It was as if the old gods were dying, and with the death of religious faith there was the decay of morality. It was indeed a decadent world. I felt despair and cynicism everywhere. Yet, I could see a kind of wistfulness in Gentile faces. I became aware again of the sharp tension between Gentile and

Jew when one day Saul and I were walking along the streets of Tarsus and I heard somebody say, "There goes that Jew boy." I went with him to his synagogue one sabbath evening and felt a flicker of hope. I noticed two or three Gentiles were attending the service, and asked Saul the meaning of this. "They are here," he said, "not seeking our God so much as our morality. There is a longing in the Gentile heart for moral purity and goodness."

Then I went to Jerusalem, and it was there that I realized how tragic the division between Jew and Gentile was. I visited the Temple, and, being a Gentile, I worshiped in the outer court where Gentile visitors were admitted. And there on that wall in bold letters, written in Greek and Latin, were these words: "No man of another race is to proceed within the partition and enclosing wall about the sanctuary; and anyone arrested there will have himself to blame for the penalty of death which will be imposed as a consequence." Rumor had it that there were those who had disregarded the warning and had paid for the violation with their lives. It was then that I knew how formidable and hostile the wall was dividing Jew and Gentile.

I remember the night I was in a reflective mood. I was thinking how hostile and divided that world was. It was so rifted. I felt as if these ghastly cleavages extended beyond mankind and history, going far out into the universe. It was as if the cosmos were cracked.

One evening, while I was in Ephesus, I attended the church there. It was not a large group, and for most part was composed of simple people. What Paul had said about the Corinthian church applied to that church, too. "For consider your call, brethren," he had written, "not many of you were wise according to worldly standards, not many were powerful, not many were of noble birth" (1 Cor. 1:26). There I found Jew and Gentile, free and slave, men and women. I couldn't believe what I was seeing and experiencing. These people loved and accepted each other. I felt an equality there that I had not found anywhere else. The old barriers were down. The old hostilities were gone. They worshiped God in joy, and, knowing he had accepted them in Christ, they were able to accept each other. I remembered the night I had worshiped in the synagogue at Tarsus and had felt hope like a flickering light shining in a dark world. That flickering light had become a dawn, and what a wonderfully fine day it was. I knew God was uniting his broken world in the church, and I felt healing was taking place out there beyond man's history.

My second sermon, "A Man Totally Saved," is about Zacchaeus. Once more I would like to enter imaginatively into the situation where Zacchaeus met Jesus.

History will not let us forget the day Jesus came to Jericho. He had passed the peak of his popularity, but was still able to inspire great crowds. He was on his last journey to Jerusalem. Many people had come to see him. They lined the road for several miles. Invalids had been laid on stretchers along the wayside, and the blind, like Bartimaeus who would not shut up calling for Jesus, were there. I was jostled in the streets by the crowds who, in their excitement, were not very polite. The atmosphere was electric with expectancy. I had the feeling that anything could happen. For a brief moment, I remembered that Jericho was one of the oldest cities in the world. This was not the first time its streets had been crowded with excited people. I envisioned generals leading victorious armies that way, trailed by captives as the chief spoil of war, who would be sold as slaves. I could see long caravans winding their way through the streets as they moved north and south. For centuries commerce had flowed along that ancient highway that ran through Jericho. It was as if the centuries looked down on us.

But one man especially caught my attention. He was a little man, Zacchaeus, who could not see over the crowds. So he had climbed up into a sycamore tree, and there he was, having forgotten his dignity, perched like a bird on a limb. He was probably the wealthiest and most despised man of the city. He administered an oppressive system of taxation in the area and the people hated him. His pretentious house built on the highest hill was a symbol of his loneliness and rejection. The names of his family were not in the social register of the city.

As a boy Zacchaeus was smaller than his friends. He could not run as fast nor climb as high as they. They nicknamed him "shorty," and that name burned in his mind like a searing iron. One day he swore beneath his breath that he would outdo all his friends. And he did! At last, he could have bought out all of them. He discovered, however, that his immense wealth could not buy what his heart most craved.

Jesus saw the little man in the sycamore tree, and violated a social propriety: He invited himself to have lunch with Zacchaeus. Jesus never allowed social propriety to stand between him and people who needed him. That day at lunch Jesus did for him what his money never could have done. Jesus gave him new life. Zacchaeus was saved, and there was no fragmentation in the salvation that Jesus gave. His total life was redeemed. He said to Jesus: "Behold, Lord, the half of my goods I give to the poor; and if I have defrauded any one of anything, I restore it fourfold" (Luke 19:8).

The word got around. The hearts of mothers, who had put their children to bed hungry the night before, leaped up. Some of Zacchaeus's wealth might reach them. Zacchaeus went uptown that day and surprised many men whom he had cheated. To one he gave ten pounds, to another twenty-five, to another fifty, and still another one hundred. Many others were the recipients of this unexpected generosity. He was as good as his word—he was restoring fourfold.

Zacchaeus's soul was saved. But that was not all. His social and economic relations were transformed. The value of human faces went up, while the value of the pound went down. His whole life was redeemed.

WHAT NOW?

The questions, what then? and what now? are really hermeneutical questions. Hermeneutics, as earlier suggested, is concerned with the authentic interpretation of Scripture in such a way that its truth speaks to us today. We have to ask how we can translate an ancient text into the language and life context of the last quarter of the twentieth century.

It is not enough to do an accurate exegetical study of the text and then enter the historical situation imaginatively. Another step has to be taken: The truth has to be transposed so it can speak to the needs and demands of today's life. Those of us who preach can take heart: The ancient bibilical word is transposable into the life of the late twentieth century.

Let me take the two sermons in which I reentered the historical situation imaginatively and show how the ancient texts can speak to our life today. I will be answering the question: What now?

The first sermon is "Healing the Rift." The Scripture lesson is Ephesians 1:1-10, the text is Ephesians 1:10.

Paul believed that the great tragedy of human existence is that life is broken, divided, and rifted. The rift lies not only across man and his history but extends into the cosmos. It is as if the cosmos is broken. But a secret, long hidden, is now revealed: God is healing and uniting all things, in history and beyond history, in Christ. It is God's purpose "as a plan for the fulness of time, to unite all things in him, things in heaven and things on earth" (Eph. 1:10).

How can that ancient text speak to us today? It can speak to us because we face the same tragedy that Paul was so acutely aware of, and we cling to his hope.

John McKay, past president of Princeton Theological Seminary, has written: "The universe is rifted. History and the heart of men are rifted. The fact of this rift is the elemental, decisive fact about reality in its wholeness."[3]

There are barriers that still divide us. Life is rifted. It is like a torn garment, like a rent piece of fabric.

Our world is divided between East and West. The Communist and free worlds are in conflict. Race is set against race, nation against nation, and class against class. We even speak of the schizophrenic person who has a split personality.

The split on the human and historical level doesn't seem adequate to explain our tragedy. The cosmos seems to be split.

I visited Dachau, one of Hitler's infamous concentration camps, in 1970. Almost twenty-five years had passed since Dachau had been taken by the Allied forces and its prisoners set free. And, as if in a kind of effort to redeem the place, three chapels—Jewish, Catholic, and Protestant—had been erected. Still, a terrible power of evil seemed to hover over that place. What could be the source of that evil? I thought of the German heart and the German social structure. While there was evil in both, these didn't seem adequate to explain the terrible darkness that settled over Dachau. It seemed as if a dreadful evil had come from above that place, engulfing it. Or to use our imagery: There was a split in the German heart, a rift in the German social order, and there was a split that lay beyond the German heart and German society.

I remember a nursery rhyme I learned as a child:

Humpty Dumpty sat on a wall,
Humpty Dumpty had a great fall;
All the King's horses and all the King's men
Cannot put Humpty Dumpty together again.

Our existence, like Humpty Dumpty, has had a great fall, and "All the King's horses and all the King's men" cannot put our world together again. All our science, technology, know-how, and knowledge cannot put our world together again.

Must we give up in despair? Is there anybody who can help us? Is there anyone who can overcome our splitness? Is there anyone who can heal the rift? Yes, God can. That is the kind of action he has taken in Jesus Christ. He plans to heal our brokenness, overcome our splitness, and unite us in Christ. Where does he want this to happen? In the church which is the body of Christ. Does it really happen? Yes. Maybe not as often as we would like, but when it does occur we know how wonderful it is. And God will heal the cosmos.

My second sermon is "A Man Totally Saved." The Scripture lesson is Luke 19:1-10, my text, Luke 19:9.

This sermon is concerned with the story of Zacchaeus which can certainly speak to us in our time.

Our world is full of Zacchaeuses—men and women of overweening ambition who seek wealth and power, and having achieved these, feel lonely, isolated, empty, and unfulfilled. They discover, often too late, that their wealth and power cannot get for them the things their hearts long for.

Zacchaeus may have been much better than the system he served. The tax system he administered was oppressive and therefore evil. But because it offered him security and met his enormous drive for power, he stifled the better impulses of his heart. He excused himself and rationalized what he was doing. He got caught in the clutches of the system. The same thing happens to many of us. It is so easy to get caught in systems, in corporate life, that blunt our ideals and dull our consciences. We sell our souls for success over which lies a shadow.

Further, our culture is a mirror in which the Zacchaeuses of our time can see their faces. Our culture honors status symbols and for these we work our fingers to the bone. The fact that we seek so desperately for status symbols which are external tells us how empty we are on the inside. We know the inner bankruptcy that Zacchaeus also knew.

Is there help for the modern Zacchaeus? Yes, the Christ who saved the Zacchaeus of our Scripture lesson can save us. He is as eager to get to us as he was to Zacchaeus. He crosses barriers much more formidable than social propriety. And, when he gets to us, he is not willing to save just our souls. He wants to save the total life in its total setting. He wants to redeem all our relationships.

We who preach must take a step backward into the biblical world where we see God's mighty action and hear his powerful voice. Then we must take a step forward into the modern world, bringing with us the Word of God. We must ask, what then? and we must ask, what now?

12
The Appeal of the Evangel's Voice

Evangelistic preaching is the kind we should do first. If one has a broken arm, the first thing one does is to have it set. Only then can normal healing take place. Only then can the arm be straight and useful again.

If one has a broken relationship with God, the first thing is to help heal that relationship. Only then can one be spiritually strong and healthy. Evangelistic preaching knows the sources of healing.

Evangelistic preaching is basically what we find in the New Testament. God's saving events in the past are declared. Then, against that background, the greatest of God's saving deeds, the Christ event, is proclaimed. Salvation is offered and people are asked to repent, believe, and be baptized into the church.

Until we do evangelistic preaching well, all other kinds will be shallow, even futile. Until new life is given, there is no life worthy of cultivation.

WHAT IS EVANGELISTIC PREACHING?

Let me suggest that in evangelistic preaching three things are done.

First, good news is announced.

Our word *evangelism* comes from the Greek, *euangelion*, which means good news. The evangel is one who announces the

179

good news of God's redemption in Christ. That good news is like saying to a lost person, "There are the lights of home"; to a person in bondage, "You can be free"; to a hungry man, "There is bread"; to a blind man, "You can see again"; to a sick man, "You can be well again"; to a dying man, "You can live." When the evangel's voice is clear and authentic, there is no voice nearly as appealing. He has good news in a world where news seems to be predominantly bad.

Frederick Buechner's Lyman Beecher Lectures of 1977 were published under the title: *Telling the Truth: The Gospel as Tragedy, Comedy, and Fairy Tale.* He does a very interesting thing. He puts theological truth into literary categories.

Buechner says that the gospel is bad news before it is good news. The bad news is that man is a sinner, that he has lost his way. That is the gospel as tragedy. But it is also the news that he is loved anyway, cherished, forgiven. Against a long dark night, the coming of morning is announced. It is such good news that we feel like laughing. That is the gospel as comedy. Beyond that, extraordinary things happen: things you would not expect, things you could not anticipate. It is too good to be true, yet it is true. That is the gospel as fairy tale.

I would like to return to Jesus' three great parables recorded in the fifteenth chapter of Luke: The Lost Sheep, The Lost Coin, and The Lost Son. They all begin with a tragic note: Something is lost. That is the bad news of the gospel. The good news of the gospel is always announced against the long night with its heavy overcast and starless sky. Then something is sought. The shepherd seeks his lost sheep, the woman her lost coin, and the lost son his father's house. It is like the watchman announcing to those of the long night: "Look! Light is breaking in the east, morning is coming." Finally, something is found. The sheep is back in the fold, the coin is back in the purse, and the boy is back home. So the morning breaks into full day, and what a splendid day it is!

Second, something is called for. Let me suggest four things.

In the first place, repentance is called for. Mark introduced Jesus' great Galilean ministry like this: "Now after John was arrested, Jesus came into Galilee, preaching the gospel of God, and saying; 'The time is fulfilled, and the kingdom of God is at hand; repent, and believe in the gospel'" (Mark 1:14). That was indeed good news. The kingdom of God was breaking in upon their time. They could not be passive in the face of something so momentous. They must be responsive, and the first thing they had to do was to repent. But what is repentance?

I remember pre-Easter classes I had for children ten years of age and older. They came directly from school to the church for a week, and I talked with them about the meaning of Christian faith and commitment. On Thursday we talked about repentance. When I asked them what it meant, eager hands would go up and their answers were almost invariably the same: "Repentance means to feel sorry for your sins." That is a popular way of thinking about repentance, but, while remorse is an element in it, it is not its basic meaning. To repent means to have a radical change of heart, mind, and will. One's life turns from old ways into new ones. The face is set in a new direction, and feet walk in new paths.

Judas Iscariot was shocked and depressed when he heard that Pilate had sentenced Jesus to death. He never dreamed that his betrayal of Jesus would be a part of such drastic and tragic action. If he could have called back just a few hours, he would not have done it. He took the thirty pieces of silver, the price of a slave, that had been given him for his dastardly act, and brought them to the religious leaders in the Temple. He confessed that he had betrayed innocent blood, and they, in a most heartless way, said to him: "What is that to us? See to it yourself" (Matt. 27:4). He scattered the coins on the floor of the Temple, and went out into the night and hanged himself. Although Matthew tells us "he repented" (Matt. 27:3), repentance led to no change of life. Judas Iscariot only felt remorseful about his treacherous deed, and his remorse plunged him more deeply into the darkness of his despair.

A friend and I several years ago drove to Princeton Theological Seminary for a summer conference. We decided that we would drive up the beautiful Shenandoah Valley of Virginia and pick up US Highway 1 in Philadelphia. This we did. We had driven for twenty miles when one of us remarked that we had not seen a sign to Trenton, and about that time we noticed one pointing to Baltimore. We were headed wrong. We might have continued in that direction, feeling remorseful that we had made the wrong turn in Philadelphia, but we would never have reached our destination. Remorse would not have changed the situation. We turned around, headed north, retracing our steps. When that kind of radical turnabout happens in our moral and spiritual life, authentic repentance occurs. Only that kind of repentance puts us in touch with moral and spiritual reality that alone can make possible the new life.

Again, faith is called for.

As already stated, faith is more than intellectual assent to propositional truths. We have to be more than philosophers, seeking to rid ourselves of all religious bias and look out upon life and our world with clear and objective eyes, trying to find evidence for and against God, and finally concluding that a preponderance of evidence points toward God. But that can never be saving faith. Faith is more than declaring: "I hold these truths to be valid."

Yet, we are tempted to accept faith as intellectual assent. I remember an old man who turned philosopher at the close of day at a country store in eastern North Carolina. It was dusk and the stars were coming out when he said: "You can't see the stars come out at night and not believe in God." Yet, he came to the end of his life not having made a confession of saving faith.

James made a very startling observation in this regard:

"You believe that God is one; you do well. Even demons believe—and shudder" (Jas. 2:19). Demons believe, but remain demonic. They look out upon a universe that bears unmistakable evidence of a creator, and they shudder before the awesomeness of God. They intellectually acknowledge the reality of God. Yet, they are not changed. They remain fiendish.

What is the faith we are called upon to exercise? It is trust in and surrender to Jesus Christ. It is forsaking our self-centered, self-seeking way of life which fails us at last, and getting onto the sure and unfailing grace of God in Christ. We are like a pilot bailing out of a plane that has been shot from beneath him. He sees the rocky earth to which he is falling. Death is certain unless something can break the fall. He pulls the cord of his parachute, trusting it alone to save him. His faith is not misplaced. The parachute gently wafts him to earth. In such a manner we trust Christ for salvation. We trust him and him alone.

There are those who believe that the central concern of religion is with salvation. In the light of this, the claim could be made that the Philippian jailer asked Paul and Silas the most basic religious question: "Men, what must I do to be saved?" (Acts 16:30). They gave him the most basic answer to his question: "Believe in the Lord Jesus, and you will be saved, you and your household" (Acts 16:31).

Further, confession is called for.

We make confession in two senses: We confess our sins to Christ as Savior, and then we confess him before men as Lord.

I remember on many first Sunday mornings standing at our communion table and saying: "If we confess our sins, he is faithful and just, and will forgive our sins and cleanse us from all unrighteousness" (1 John 1:9). It is such a wonderful privilege to say that. Christ is as good as his word: He does forgive us when we confess our sins to him.

Only Christ can forgive sins. I have done a lot of counseling over a rather long ministry. I have heard many seamy stories told with guilt and shame, all of which I have been careful to keep in confidence. But I have never been able to say: "I forgive you." I have to leave that to Christ.

One pastor remembers a doctor calling him and telling him about a patient who felt so guilty that she didn't want to live. This was frustrating the doctor's attempt to help her get well. He confessed that this problem was beyond his skill. Would the pastor see the patient? Within a half hour, the patient was in the pastor's study. She told him that she had broken all of the Ten Commandments, except one. She had never murdered anyone. The pastor assured her that the grace of Christ is greater than all our sins, and no matter what she had done Christ could and would forgive her if she would accept his forgiveness. This she gladly did and, with her confession and acceptance of Christ's grace, new zest for life was given her. She wanted to live again. The doctor called the pastor a few weeks later, telling him he wanted to report that his patient's progress in getting well was almost miraculous.

We are to confess Christ before men. "Because, if you confess with your lips that Jesus is Lord," Paul wrote, "and believe in your heart that God raised him from the dead, you will be saved. For man believes with his heart and so is justified, and he confesses with his lips and so is saved" (Rom. 10:9-10).

We make a public confession by presenting ourselves for church membership and being baptized. Our life is under new management, and we are glad for people to know it. We have a new Lord, a new center, a new scale of values, and a new direction. We make the confession of the Lordship of Christ by a new life-style. At the heart of this new life-style is *agape* love. "By this all men will know that you are my disciples," Jesus said, "if you have love for one another" (John 13:35).

I remember the Sunday night I baptized four laymen all of whom were in their fifties. They had been won by other laymen who had borne their witness very insecurely. But God had greatly blessed their awkward ways. One of the men who had been baptized said to me as he left the church: "This is the end of a perfect day." He had been glad to acknowledge Christ as his Lord.

Finally, membership in the family or community of Christ, which is the church, is called for.

Christian faith is very personal. Christ loves me and he forgives me. Although it could not be more personal, it is never private. It is social. We need others. We need the church.

It never occurred to the early church to leave a new believer outside its fellowship. That would have been like leaving a newborn baby outside his family. For example, those who were converted at Pentecost immediately became members of the church. "So those who received his word were baptized," according to the account, "and there were added that day about three thousand souls. And they devoted themselves to the apostles' teaching and fellowship, to the breaking of bread and the prayers" (Acts 2:41).

We have too often considered the church as a kind of appendage of the gospel, an afterthought. But the church is part of the good news. Paul visited many of the great cities of his world. He came with the gospel to those cities and always left behind him a church as he moved on. The good news was not only that Paul came with the gospel, but that when he moved on he left behind him a church. Christianity could not have survived in that world without those churches that supported, nurtured, and matured the believers in Christ. Beyond that, they kept alive the memory of Jesus Christ and inspired the writing of the New Testament. And oddly enough, the best claim to fame for many of those cities was that a little church was somewhere in its life and that an itinerant preacher by the name of Paul wrote letters to them. Those cities may have not known that, but history knows it, and for millions of people in our world some of those ancient cities are remembered only because they are mentioned in Paul's letters.

Third, something is promised.

We are promised new relationships and new life.

As has been said earlier, relationships are the very essence of life. Without them we cannot live. The tragedy of life can be explained in terms of broken relationships, while salvation can be expressed in terms of broken relationships made whole. It is little wonder then that the Bible thinks in relational terms and the basic Christian vocabulary is composed almost solely of relational words.

The tragedy of life is that we are separated from God and alienated from our brother. We are cut off from God who is the basic spring of life and from our brother who is the secondary spring. For this reason the Bible thinks of death in broader terms than the physical and biological failure of life, and can speak of persons as being dead while they still live. We can continue with biological life after we have been cut off from the springs of life.

The good news of the evangel is that these broken relationships can be healed, that our lives can be put in touch again with the springs of life. We don't have to remain separated from God and alienated from the brother. We can be reconciled to both. And in the midst of death, we can have eternal life that comes from a new relationship with God that can never be broken. Paul knew how weak and fragile the relationships of life are. In the closing part of the eighth chapter of Romans, he runs the full gamut of vicissitude and tragedy that leaves so many of our relationships in shambles and concludes that nothing "will be able to separate us from the love of God in Christ Jesus our Lord" (Rom. 8:39). Eternal life is bound up with that relationship that will not fail us.

Paul understood God's primary mission in Jesus Christ as being that of reconciliation. "God was in Christ," Paul wrote, "reconciling the world unto himself" (2 Cor. 5:19, KJV). I have known theology and preaching that said in effect that it was God who needed to be reconciled to his world. Paul said just the opposite—not God, but the world was in need of reconciliation.

We must not forget that God has made possible a double reconciliation. We are reconciled with God and the brother. It is both personal and social, spiritual and ethical. As a matter of fact, the New Testament makes the staggering claim that reconciliation with the brother is proof that we have been reconciled with God. "We know we have passed from death unto life." wrote John, "because we love the brethren" (1 John 3:14, KJV). Or again, "If any one says, 'I love God,' and hates his brother, he is a liar; for he who does not love his brother whom he has seen, cannot love God whom he has not seen. And this commandment we have from him, that he who loves God should love his brother also" (1 John 4:20-21). We should not forget the social dimension of reconciliation.

If God's primary mission in Jesus Christ was reconciliation, then that must be the church's basic thrust in the world. We go on a mission of reconciliation. In some real sense, we take Christ's place in the world. Imagine it! "So we are ambassadors for Christ, God making his appeal through us" (2 Cor. 5:20). God has given us the word of reconciliation to speak: "entrusting to us the message of reconciliation" (2 Cor. 5:19). The message of the evangel is "you don't have to die in your separation and estrangement; you can be returned to your source of life." We have been given a ministry of reconciliation: "And gave us the ministry of reconciliation" (2 Cor. 5:18). We are to do deeds of reconciliation in the world.

Out of these new relations comes new life. Isn't that what we need and isn't that what we really want? We are satiated with the new: New fads, new fashions, new models, new faces, new places, new experiences, new breakthroughs in science, and new frontiers crossed, but we cling to our old lives. We handle new things with old hands and we look on new things through old eyes. Is it any wonder that the new becomes old so soon? What we really need is new life and new life has been promised us.

We remember Jesus meeting the famed jurist, Nicodemus, at night, maybe on the outskirts of the city. Jesus said to him: "Truly, truly, I say to you, unless one is born anew, he cannot see the kingdom of God. . . . Do not marvel that I said to you, 'you must be born anew.' The wind blows where it will, and you hear the sound of it, but you do not know whence it comes or whither it goes; so it is with every one who is born of the Spirit" (John 3:3, 7-8). We are shocked! If Nicodemus had been a bum or criminal, we would not have been surprised. He was the finest flower of his religion and culture. He was one of those rare men who stands in the present, bearing the best of the past into the future. He was a fine, cultured gentleman by any standard. If Nicodemus needed to be born again, then we all need it. We need new life and new life is offered us by Christ.

Paul has affirmed this. "Therefore, if any one is in Christ, he is a new creation," he wrote, "the old has passed away, behold, the new has come" (2 Cor. 5:17). Paul was not theorizing or speculating. He was telling about something that had happened to him. He had become a new man in Christ. He had met the living Christ along the Damascus road. Being overpowered by the awe and wonder of it, he had fallen to the ground with his face in the dust, and had stood to his feet a new person.

Augustine, who has possibly influenced Christian theology more than any other person since Paul, was a very profligate and immoral young man. He was the kind of fellow who had a girl in every town. But his conversion changed all of that. Like Paul, he became a new creation in Christ. One day along the streets of a city, he met a former lover. She rushed toward Augustine expecting him to take her into his arms, but he rebuffed her. She backed away, looking quizzically at him, and asked: "Aren't you Augustine?" "Yes," came the reply, "but I am not the Augustine you knew. I am a new man."

What about this new life? Does it come suddenly and dramatically? Or does it come quietly and less dramatically? As said earlier, it comes both ways. Paul could have taken one to the outskirts of Damascus, told one the day and the date, and then pointing to a spot along the wayside said: "It happened here at noonday." He knew the place, the day, and the hour. But others, whose experience of grace is just as authentic as was Paul's, can't be so specific. Their experience has been more like the coming of morning. When did night become day? Well, there is the official time, but what if on a particular day there is a heavy overcast? It is still dark when light is supposed to be breaking. Day comes officially but not actually. When the mist has been lifted from the hills, the shadows driven from the valleys, and the landscape is bathed in light, we know morning has come. Just when, we cannot be sure, but that it has come there can be no dispute. So may be the working of grace, bringing us new life.

COMMON MISTAKES

We can make serious mistakes in evangelistic preaching which, one fears, are very common. Let me mention three of these.

First, the failure to declare a full salvation that saves the whole life.

We often speak of saving souls. That would be fine if we use the term soul to mean the whole life, but unfortunately that is not what we always mean. We frequently mean the spiritual side of life, the eternal spark that is within us, but that is not biblical faith. Rather, it is a Greek heresy. For the Greeks, salvation meant the freeing of the soul from the body which was its prison. The soul was divine, while the body was evil and unworthy.

Many of us are still under the influence of that Greek heresy. I have heard people say things like this: "What is important is the soul, the body really doesn't matter." Or, "This life is a kind of threshold of eternity. It is preparation for the next life." But even a scant knowledge of the Bible will let us know that it doesn't read that way. The whole life is important, not just the soul, and the whole life is to be redeemed. The spiritual life is to be set right with God, the mind is to be saved from prejudice and bias, the heart from hatred and hostility, and the will from lethargy and cowardice. Even the body is to be saved, and our redemption will not be complete until "this mortal shall have put on immortality" (1 Cor. 15:54, KJV). We are to be given new bodies. Relationships are important and they are to be transformed. Our social, political, and economic relationships are all to be made different. Our historical time is important. God thought it was important enough to send his Son into it. It was there that the incarnation took place. Our history is to be redeemed. It will be caught up into an order free from sin that has marred all our human existence. All creation will at last be redeemed. There will at last come a new heaven and a new earth.

Second, we often have not emphasized the church sufficiently. We have been so busy getting the baby born that we have often neglected the family into which he should be born. The baby can't make it without his family and the newborn Christian can't make it without the church which is the family of Christ. There he is to be loved, affirmed, nurtured, and matured in Christ.

We need to keep two things in mind. First, while the church can't save us, we could not have been saved without it. We would never have heard the good news of the gospel. No one would have told us that Jesus Christ came into the world to save sinners. It is true there is no salvation by the church. But there is no salvation without the church. And that is also true. Second, we cannot be spiritually healthy, cannot grow and mature in Christ, except as we belong to the church. Without the church we experience stunted and arrested growth. We become spiritual midgets and spiritual dwarfs. There is a sense in which we die spiritually.

Water is the habitat of fish. Take a fish out of a stream, and it may flounce around with a lot of vigor and vitality. But it is a flounce of death. It can't survive unless it can get back into the water. A Christian is like a fish in this sense. The church is his habitat, and he can't make it apart from the life of the church.

Paul's favorite metaphor for the church was the body of Christ. Just as limbs and organs make up the body, so believers in Christ make up his body which is the church. No limb or organ can survive apart from the body. To be separated from the body is to die. My hand could say to my body, "I don't like you," and my body replies, "that may be true but you can't make it without me. If you ever get separated from me you will die. You'll have to tag along with me."

If a Christian sustains the same kind of relationship with the church that the hand does to the body, then we dare not minimize the church in evangelism. The following steps are necessary as one responds to the gospel: One must repent, believe, and be baptized into the church. Baptism should be followed by a long nurturing process.

Third, we have often neglected the social dimension of evangelism.

In evangelistic preaching we need to be aware that the gospel is spiritual and ethical, personal and social. We have often neglected the social and ethical demands.

I remember the evangelism I knew as a boy in eastern North Carolina. The annual revival occurred in late August. It was a week the entire community looked forward to and it was both social and religious. We didn't do much work during that time. We visited neighbors, entertained them, and were entertained by them. Young people courted on the church grounds.

But it was an intensely religious week. I recall the fervor with which the evangelists preached and how my heart leaped up when those preachers told me that I didn't have to die in my sins. God had acted in such a way in Christ that I could be forgiven and saved. That was indeed good news and there is no evangelism unless that gospel is proclaimed. But those evangelists forgot to tell me that the Christ who sets my life right with God also sets my life right with my brother. And that has been a grievous fault that I have known in a lot of evangelism.

There is fervent but spurious evangelism that flourishes in a lot of churches. From the youngest to the oldest the members will tell you that the purpose of the church is to save souls. And often those churches that are so ardently evangelistic are at the same time the most socially blind and least concerned about social justice. I remember such a church that sent out a fleet of buses every Sunday morning over a radius of forty miles. They brought people by the bus loads and their main business was to save their souls. Yet, that church operated a private school within a stone's throw of the sanctuary which was racially segregated. They were fervently evangelistic and socially insensitive. They did not know the damage they did to a black child whom they turned from the doors of their school for no other reason than that his skin was black. That is likely to be an extreme example, but the tragedy is that there are many churches which, while being passionately evangelistic, are blind to social justice.

Charles G. Finney (1792-1875) could be an example for all preachers and evangelists. He was a leading figure in the famous Great Revival of 1858-59 when it was estimated that 600,000 persons were brought to Christ. He believed strongly in personal conversion. He believed, however, that evangelistic concern and social commitment should go hand in hand. He felt strongly that slaves should be set free, that slavery was one of the most iniquitous institutions of man's sinful devising. He was an abolitionist and refused communion to slaveholders. He went to Oberlin College to become a professor of theology, and later president. Oberlin College became the center of the abolitionist movement in the West and was the first college to admit women.

As preachers, our first task is to do evangelistic preaching. Let us learn to do it well and be faithful as evangels of the good news entrusted to us.

13
The Power of the Prophetic Voice

We speak about being called to be pastors and priests, but we are also called to be prophets. We are called upon to do prophetic preaching. Yet, this calling is often dimly perceived, if at all. Maybe one of the reasons we are so slow to do prophetic preaching is the fact that it is dangerous. It involves risk. If our first priority is to be safe, accepted, and popular, we will not undertake the prophetic task. The prophet in every generation has had a hard time. Jesus once addressed Jerusalem: "O Jerusalem, Jerusalem, killing the prophets and stoning those who are sent to you" (Matt. 23:37).

The prophet, often roughed up by the hands of his own generation, may be praised by succeeding generations who hear him with clearer ears and see him with more dispassionate eyes. Jesus spoke of how people built tombs to the rejected prophets, saying, "If we had lived in the days of our fathers, we would not have taken part with them in shedding the blood of the prophets" (Matt. 23:30). The prophet put down by his own generation may be easily extolled by those who follow him. Let the generations then know that they can kill a prophet but are helpless to kill his influence, can silence him but not his truth.

More than any other person, the prophet, even though dead, still speaks. The voice of the prophet is indeed a powerful one. That is true because the prophet speaks the word of God in two of its most powerful dimensions, judgment and hope.

WHAT IS PROPHETIC PREACHING?

Prophetic preaching is more than addressing social issues and appealing to human resources in solving them. It is more than speaking against injustice and then calling upon our congregation to be fair and just. People often come to worship with depleted strength and need to hear more than the preacher's demand upon the meager resources they have left. It is hard to spur people to brave and courageous action when they feel like resting by the wayside. Such preaching is too horizontal, it is too flat. A steady diet of such preaching can dry up the pulpit and empty the pews. People have dimensions of height and depth to which such preaching cannot speak. We need the vertical dimension, to feel height and mystery, and to hear a word that comes from beyond us. We need to feel depth. A spiritual shaft has been struck deep inside the human heart. There are hopes, longings, and desires that lie buried within us. There are deep interior springs that the gospel needs to replenish so they can flow again. We need to slake our spiritual thirst at springs that do not fail. Preaching that moves along the horizontal line cannot do that. There are heights it cannot reach and depths it cannot touch.

But you would misunderstand me if you hear me saying that social issues are not to be addressed. They are. Prophetic preaching is concerned with social issues, with our corporate, collective, and institutional life. But we address these realities not simply as moralist or social analysts. We address them as prophets to whom God has given a word to speak. In prophetic preaching we bring our corporate life beneath the word of God, both in its judgment and its hope, both in its wounding and its healing. When we speak the word of God, there is the vertical dimension. The word comes from beyond us. But because the word has hope in it, it has a depth dimension. It offers forgiveness and healing.

The word of God is given to the prophet. In a sense, this is what sets him apart and makes him unique. Jeremiah said "the Lord put forth his hand and touched my mouth, and the Lord said to me, 'Behold, I have put my words in your mouth./See, I have set you this day over nations and over kingdoms/to pluck up and to break down,/to destroy and to overthrow/to build and to plant'" (Jer. 1:9-10).

I have spoken of the power of the prophetic voice. Note the imagery in Jeremiah's call to be a prophet. God was setting him over nations and kingdoms. He was to pluck up and break down, to destroy and overthrow, to build and to plant. We are left almost reeling under the heavy blows of those powerful metaphors.

Or take Amos. He said to Amaziah the priest: "I am no prophet, nor a prophet's son; but I am a herdsman, and a dresser of sycamore trees, and the Lord took me from following the flock, and the Lord said to me, 'Go, prophesy to my people Israel'" (Amos 7:14-15). This simple rustic man was sent forth with a word from God on his lips. And what a word it was!

Now this word has judgment in it as already indicated. Amos began his prophecy by telling of God's judgment coming down heavily on the surrounding nations who were Israel's enemies. Israel exulted in this. Then like a bolt of lightning, Amos told Israel, the people of God, that they were not being spared. God's judgment was coming down shatteringly on them: "Hear this word that the Lord has spoken against you, O people of Israel, against the whole family which I brought up out of the land of Egypt: You only have I known/of all the families of the earth;/therefore I will punish you for all your iniquities" (Amos 3:1).

Remember how Amos pictured God standing with a plumbline in his hands, dropping it along the crooked walls of Israel's life. And God was saying: "Behold, I am setting a plumbline in the midst of my people Israel. I will never again pass by them; the high places of Isaac shall be made desolate,/and the sanctuaries of Israel shall be laid waste,/and I will rise against the house of Jeroboam" (Amos 7:8-9).

But God's judgment unrelieved is too harsh, too severe, and too devastating. There must also be spoken the word of hope and promise. Amos who envisioned God's judgment in harshest and severest terms also spoke the word of hope and promise. Hope moves like the morning against the terrible night of God's judgment. Thus Amos's book ends in hope: "I will restore the fortunes of my people Israel,/and they shall rebuild the ruined cities and inhabit them;/they shall plant vineyards and drink their wine,/and they shall make gardens and eat their fruit./I will plant them upon their land, and they shall never again be plucked up/out of the land which I have given them,/says the Lord your God" (Amos 9:14-15).

Isaiah saw his nation as being exceedingly sinful, "Ah, sinful nation,"/he cried, "a people laden with iniquity,/offspring of evildoers,/sons who deal corruptly" (Isa. 1:4). The judgment of God was sure and certain: "Your country lies desolate,/your cities are burned with fire;/in your very presence/aliens devour your land,/it is desolate, as overthrown by aliens" (Isa. 1:7). Yet, Isaiah held out hope: "Come now, let us reason together,/says the Lord:/though your sins are like scarlet, they shall be as white as snow;/though they are red like crimson, they shall become like wool" (Isa. 1:18).

Since prophetic preaching is addressed to the corporate life, it should be pointed out that we are more sinful in our corporate life than in our personal relationships.

We do without the lash of conscience in our corporate life which would be unbearably painful in our personal lives. Reinhold Niebuhr talked about moral man and immoral society. We are normally much more moral individually than we are corporately.

For example, a man in a big corporation may do things that he would not do to his neighbor. As a part of the corporation he may engage in graft, kickbacks, and price fixing. He may promote advertising which is little more than clever lying, and he may be a part of a ruthless effort to destroy a competitor. Yet, in his neighborhood he is a kind, generous, and truthful man. He would not injure a neighbor, since he is solicitous and caring, and he is a concerned and responsible citizen. It is almost as if he were a man with two personalities. He is one kind of person in his personal and community life, another kind of person in his corporate life.

Not only are we more sinful in our corporate life, but we find it more difficult to repent. An individual may feel very urgently that he should repent, but the family, corporation, community, and state may find it almost impossible to confess guilt.

Isaiah in his transforming experience, knew both personal and collective guilt. "Woe is me! For I am lost; for I am a man of unclean lips." That is personal guilt. "And I dwell in the midst of a people with unclean lips" (Isa. 6:5). That is collective or corporate guilt. Isaiah confesses his sin and is forgiven but the nation does not.

Jesus addressing Jerusalem said: "How often would I have gathered your children together as a hen gathers her brood under her wings, and you would not" (Matt. 23:37). Individuals in Jerusalem responded to Jesus but the city did not.

Possibly history knows of no nation that confessed its guilt except in defeat. It seems to be something a nation finds impossible to do in years of power.

A fairly recent example was our crisis with Iran when they were holding some of our citizens as hostages. One of the demands Iran made at one time for the release of our citizens

was that President Carter confess our nation's guilt for being
involved in the Shah's regime and his crimes against the Iranian
people. The truth is that a nation involved in international
politics and power never comes out of it with lily-white hands.
There is always guilt. Our nation had helped put the Shah in
power and therefore had to assume some responsibility for his
misuse of it. We were not guiltless. President Carter seemed
once to make some attempt at confession in veiled language for
the nation, but he was not able to. The American people
wouldn't let him. If he had, it likely would have been history's
first time to hear a great and powerful nation say it had been
wrong.

IN THE PROPHETIC TRADITION

We are in the prophetic tradition. We may wish we were not
but we are. We may prove ourselves unworthy of it, but we have
been called into it. Back of us stand the Hebrew prophets of
ancient Israel.

No figures tower so tall in Israel's history as the prophets.
Their strong voices have not been silenced by the long and
tumultous years. They have laid an indelible imprint on human
history. Their shadows lie across the landscape of our modern
world. We are still having our vision clarified by their word of
justice. We find courage in their example. They embolden us
with their heroic action. They still inspire us. How often, for
example, Amos speaks to us today: "Take away from me the
noise of your songs; to the melody of your harps I will not listen.
But let justice roll down like waters, and righteousness
like an ever-flowing stream" (Amos 5:23-24). While Amos, as
did the other prophets, spoke to a particular time, there is a
timelessness about his words. They speak to all times, and they
prick the consciences of men and women everywhere.

These were men who were concerned about justice,
compassion, and humanness. They found authority in the word

of God which had been given them.

But standing back of us is a man greater than the prophets. There can be no doubt that Jesus followed in the prophetic tradition. He talked like a prophet. He had a fresh word from God addressed to the sham, hypocrisy, and sin of his generation. He was on the side of the poor, the exploited, and the oppressed. His inaugural address which he delivered in his home synagogue had the ring and authority of the prophet: "The Spirit of the Lord is upon me, because he has anointed me to preach good news to the poor. He has sent me to proclaim release to the captives, and recovering of sight to the blind, to set at liberty those who are oppressed, to proclaim the acceptable year of the Lord" (Luke 4:18-19).

He was like an Amos upbraiding the cities along the Sea of Galilee. "Woe to you, Chorazin!" he shouted, "Woe to you Bethsaida! for if the mighty works done in you had been done in Tyre and Sidon, they would have repented long ago in sackcloth and ashes" (Matt. 11:20-21).

He said his generation was immature, fickle, and irresponsible. They were like children playing wedding and funeral in the streets whose playing had turned to petty quarreling and who were saying to one another: "We piped to you, and you did not dance;/we wailed and you did not mourn" (Matt. 11:17).

Jesus spoke his severest word to organized religion and its leaders. He saw so much sham and hypocrisy in it. The word of God had been distorted by their traditions and grace had been lost in legalism. The inwardness of religion was sacrificed to formalism, and religious leaders seemed to have lost touch with God and people. The whole system was corrupted by power. It is in his pronouncements against the religion of his day that we see what powers of irony and sarcasm he had. "Woe to you, scribes and Pharisees, hypocrites!" he cried. "For you are like whitewashed tombs, which outwardly appear beautiful, but within they are full of dead men's bones and all uncleanness. So you also outwardly appear righteous to men, but within you are fully of hypocrisy and iniquity" (Matt. 23:27-28).

Yet, like the Hebrew prophets, Jesus held out hope. "The time is fulfilled, and the kingdom of God is at hand"; he preached. "Repent, and believe in the gospel" (Mark 1:15). The kingdom of God was beating on their doors. In the light of this momentous reality Jesus called on his generation to do an about-face and believe the good news of the gospel he was proclaiming.

It is little wonder that Jesus' generation saw him as a prophet. They associated him with the greatest and the best in their religion and history. In his retreat with his disciples near Caesarea Philippi, Jesus asked them: "Who do men say that the Son of Man is?" They answered: "Some say John the Baptist, others say Elijah, and others Jeremiah or one of the prophets" (Matt. 16:13-14). On his triumphal entry into Jerusalem when the city was electric with hope and excitement, people were asking: "Who is this?" The crowds responded, "This is the prophet Jesus from Nazareth of Galilee" (Matt. 21:11).

THE NEED FOR PROPHETIC PREACHING

There are so many problems arising out of our collective and corporate life that can destroy us. In the light of this, it is nothing short of tragedy when the prophetic voice is either weak or silent in the pulpit. One wonders if any generation in history has needed more the strong, courageous voice of the prophet than does ours.

What are some of the issues we should be bringing beneath the word of God, both in judgment and hope?

We certainly should address the wild and uncontrolled armaments race. Nothing so threatens our world with bankruptcy as the mad race for arms. Not only are military weapons destructive, they are not productive economically. They devour the precious resources of our earth, and are careless of human values and welfare. One wishes one could see a greater effort toward disarmament rather than the building up of huge arsenals, a greater concern for peacemaking than preparation for war, but one does not see it. This race lies like a threatening specter across the landscape of our world.

The armament race is closely related to the possibility of nuclear war which certainly must be addressed. The horribleness and destruction of a nuclear war staggers the imagination. We can see wholesale death, our great cities lying in shambles, millions of homeless and helpless people roaming around like scavengers, the fall-out possibly affecting us so adversely genetically that our offspring will be more like monsters than humans, and our being suddenly plunged into the twilight of a dark age. Those who would survive it would envy those who died. God spare us that!

We must speak to overpopulation. We need not only to control our armaments, we need to control our human reproduction. We can so easily tax the resources of our earth beyond their power to sustain us. In a sense, we can push ourselves off our planet.

We must also address our environmental crisis to which we have earlier made reference. We have contaminated our air, polluted our streams and lakes, and often poisoned and wasted our soil. We have scarred nature's beauty and used up her resources in most profligate ways. And now nature, as if in wrath, raises an angry hand to strike down her exploiter. We need to become the responsible keepers and custodians of earth. She is the stage on which our human drama is played, the setting where our history unfolds. We are kin to nature. In a sense the earth is our good mother who nurtures and sustains us. Destroy her and we destroy ourselves. Protect her and we protect ourselves. Love her and we love ourselves.

We must be concerned with world hunger which is related to the overpopulation and environmental crises. Ours is a hungry world. There are 460 million people on our planet who are threatened with starvation. Ten million are starving each year, most of them children under ten years of age. In our shrunken world these hungry and starving people are not far from us. They are almost as close to us as the beggar Lazarus was to Dives who dressed in purple and fared sumptuously every day. It is as if they are laid at the end of our walkways. They seem to press their pinched faces against the windows of our dining rooms where we glut ourselves with rich food. They almost touch us with their thin, bony fingers. We cannot escape them in our time of history, and Jesus said we would have to face them at the end of history in the day of judgment. We need to prick the conscience of the affluent people who are overfed, overclothed, oversheltered, and overcared, and who are often unmoved by the pain of the suffering masses.

We must speak the word of judgment against racism. Wherever it raises its ugly head we are to strike it. Few things are more impoverishing and dehumanizing.

We must address our technology, making sure that it is used for worthy social ends. We must humanize it, giving it heart and compassion. We must insist that men and women, on whom our technology has lavished such gifts of power, use that power responsibly.

We must speak to the moral degeneracy of a society where moral absolutes, like anchors, have been lifted, and replaced by shifting and changing relative values. How often behavior is determined by time and place, not by the moral values that have stood the test of the ages. We need to sink again some moral absolutes, like huge shafts, into the life of our time.

We must speak to many forms of social, political, and economic injustice. We still have the oppressed, and the powerful still exploit the weak. We must not forget that the prophet is called to be a liberator.

And we dare not spare the church. We may well remember

the admonition of Peter: "For the time has come for judgment to begin with the household of God" (1 Pet. 4:17). Maybe there is where our prophetic preaching should begin.

Often the church has been little more than the extension of its culture. It has used religious language but the raucous voice of secularism could be heard. It has dressed in religious garb but its robes have been so sheer that its worldly values could be seen. We have often been like the church of Laodicea which could boast: "I am rich, I have prospered, and I need nothing." But Christ said to that church: "You are wretched, pitiable, poor, blind, and naked" (Rev. 3:17). The church had prospered but its success was like that of the city. It had taken into its life the values of the community and baptized them in the name of Jesus Christ. It was more like a chamber of commerce advertising the culture of the city than a redemptive fellowship with a message of hope which often contradicted the values of the culture. That church could neither be prophetic nor redemptive.

I can remember how shocked I was in the sixties when someone said: "The 11 o'clock hour on Sunday morning is the most segregated hour of the week." It was true then, and it is true now. It is so tragic that racism made one of its last-ditch fights in the church. Often today it is doing a rear-guard action there.

The church has a wonderful treasure in its book, the Bible. It is essentially a book of liberation. Yet, I think of how often the church has used it as a book of oppression and is still doing so. Has not Christ as fully liberated women as he has men, and has he not given to women every gift he has made to men? Yet, many churches falsely use the Bible as an oppressive tool keeping women in spiritual bondage. Many churches will not ordain women as deacons and still more will not ordain them as ministers. This is really a negation of our gospel of liberation. Judgment does indeed need to begin at the household of God.

Yet, a strong word of caution should be given. Everything

is not bad in our society and everything is not wrong in our churches. There is much good in both. We have a lot of hard-won values in our culture which we need to affirm and support. The church often has spiritual vision, moral courage, and social sensitivity. We have spoken of racism in the church, but we must remember that a large part of the vanguard that went forth to redress racial wrongs came from our churches.

And we should always speak a word of hope. When there is repentance and faith, there can be forgiveness, renewal, and new beginnings. This is God's world and he is always seeking to redeem it. History is where he meets us, telling us who he is, and he will see that history is consummated, ending the way it should. We do not lose heart.

SURVIVING PROPHETIC PREACHING

Prophetic preaching is dangerous. It can be painfully disruptive. Pastors and churches are often injured. For this reason we are tempted not to do it.

Prophetic preaching touches sensitive and controversial issues. We are tempted to avoid addressing these issues by preaching about historical, ethereal, and future reality. These are all a part of our gospel. Christianity is a historical religion and Jesus Christ is back of us in history. Wonder and mystery are above us, and the second coming of Christ when he will consummate history lies out ahead of us. But to preach about what is back of us, what is above us, and what is ahead of us in a way so that we do not have to confront the painful issues of today is to distort our gospel. It is a copout.

Yet, the fact remains: prophetic preaching is dangerous. How does one do it and survive? That is an important question. Let me make three suggestions.

First, we have to be both priest and prophet; that is to say, we have to be both pastor and prophet. The priest and prophet usually don't like each other. Remember, Amaziah, the priest of

Bethel, saying to Amos, the itinerant prophet: "O seer, go, flee away to the land of Judah, and eat bread there, and prophesy there" (Amos 7:12). The presence of the prophet was too threatening; therefore the two men were instantly in conflict with each other. When the priest and the prophet meet in the life of the preacher they still don't like each other. Thus the pastor who would be both priest and prophet must live his life under tension. But he must be willing to live with this tension if he is to be a prophet that heals rather than destroys. If only a priest, he will never be a prophet. If only a prophet, his ministry will be disruptive. We have to be both.

Second, we must create relationships with sufficient depth to absorb the shock and tension of prophetic preaching. This requires a lot of loving pastoral care and it demands time. It takes time to establish those deep relationships that can stand the stress of the prophetic voice. There are many supporting reasons for a long pastorate, and one of the basic ones is that it gives time to create those relationships that make possible a prophetic ministry.

When a pastor has remained with his people a long time, ministering to them in love, sharing their joys and sorrows, being with them in crises such as sickness and death, baptizing them, marrying them, being their confidant and counselor, a relationship is created that can stand a lot of stress and strain. Such a pastor can also be a prophet, and the relationship can absorb the shock of the prophetic word.

During the sixties a pastor got in trouble over the racial issue. He didn't discuss racial discrimination as it existed in South Africa or some other faraway place. He would have been safe in doing that. Rather, he chose to preach about the racial situation as it existed in his community and his church. He kept telling his people that the church cannot be the church of Jesus Christ if it turns from its door people whom Christ has loved and accepted and for whom he died. The doors of the church must be as wide as the arms of its Lord. But his church, more conditioned by its culture than the mind of Christ, took offense. One night the deacons called a secret meeting to discuss the matter. The conversation was moving to what seemed to be the inevitable conclusion when one deacon stood up and said: "I cannot vote against my pastor. He sat up with my wife and me all night long during her last illness." Because of a deep relationship with one man the pastor was spared drastic action and was allowed to continue his prophetic ministry in a church and community that needed him so badly.[1]

Third, you have to do confessional preaching.

We are all caught up in the sinful structures of our world. That includes the pastor. Therefore, he does not do his prophetic preaching as a judge over other men and women. He does it as one who stands beneath the judgment of God, confessing his own sin of complicity in the world and church. He stands there as one who is judged along with other people. There should be those psychological moments when the preacher leaves his pulpit and goes into the pew, confessing his own sin along with his people. But he also stands before them as one who hopes. He knows there is forgiveness and healing.

Karl Barth said in a sermon preached to prisoners in Basel, Switzerland: "I confess being the greatest sinner among you." Only as we are willing to do that can we do prophetic preaching that is healing and not wounding.

There is a very sad word in the seventy-fourth Psalm: "We do not see our signs;/there is no longer any prophet,/and there is none among us who knows how long" (Ps. 74:9).

Let it not be said of our time: "There is no longer any prophet." Let's you and me be that prophet.

14
The Nurturing of the Pastoral Voice

The pastoral voice is nurturing. It helps make possible growth and maturity in the Christian life. Pastoral preaching and evangelistic preaching go hand in hand. They complement each other. Evangelistic preaching offers the great hope that Christ can give us new life, that we can become new creations in Christ. But what if the new life that Christ gives does not grow, what if we remain infantile? If evangelistic preaching is confident of the new life, pastoral preaching is just as confident that the new life can grow and mature. To this end pastoral preaching is committed.

THE PASTORAL ROLE

The pastoral role is crucially important. Until we fill it well, all of our other roles will suffer and be greatly impaired.

Jesus' last face-to-face meeting with Simon Peter was at the Sea of Galilee in the early morning. After breakfast, Jesus and Peter strolled along those shores that were haunted by so many pleasant memories. Jesus, three years earlier, had called him from his boat and fishing nets there. Peter had frequently come back since so much of the great Galilean ministry had centered in Capernaum. This would be an extremely crucial meeting. Jesus asked Peter: "Simon, son of John do you love me more than these?" (John 21:15). He asked this question not once, but twice, even three times, always getting a positive reply. Peter's third answer was particularly strong and emphatic: "Lord, you know everything; you know that I love you" (v. 17). Jesus' response to Peter was "Feed my lambs," and twice, "Feed my sheep" (vv. 15-17, KJV). Jesus' great concern became obvious: He wanted Peter to be a good pastor. Jesus no doubt had many hopes for Peter, but above all the rest was his concern about Peter's role as a pastor.

Maybe if Christ should share with us his deepest concern for us it might well be the same. He wants us to be good pastors.

As has already been said, the pastoral role is extremely important. In a sense, it is the foundation of all other roles in a minister's life. Whatever we do, we should do pastorally, even administration. That, more than anything else, saves administration from being tedious and boring.

Reinhold Niebuhr, when he became a minister, found the pastoral ministry, especially visiting, very difficult, but increasingly he felt its importance and fulfillment. When he resigned his pastorate in 1928 to become a professor, he wrote: "Now that the time has come to sever my connections with the church, I find it almost impossible to take the step. There is nothing quite like the pastoral relationship. I would almost be willing to sacrifice the future for the sake of staying here and watching the lovely little kiddies grow up, to see the young boys and girls I have confirmed blossoming into manhood and womanhood."[1]

At a preaching seminar at Princeton Theological Seminary in 1977, several of us had lunch one day with two girls who were theological students. One of the girls had come out of the Riverside Church in New York City, and she was lamenting the fact that Dr. Ernest Campbell had resigned as pastor of that church. She spoke of the excellence of his preaching. Then she said: "There was a pastoral dimension about Dr. Campbell's preaching. He knew how to interpret the gospel in terms of the needs of the people at Riverside." That was what had impressed her most.

There is a mistaken idea about the pastoral role. It is what you do outside the pulpit. It is visitation, counseling, crisis ministry. But these do not exhaust the possibilities of the pastoral role. We are still pastors in the pulpit, and the entire service of worship, from the invocation to the benediction, should be infused with the pastoral spirit. Whatever we do, should be done pastorally. That certainly includes the pulpit.

WHAT IS PASTORAL PREACHING?

Pastoral preaching is supportive, affirming, caring, accepting preaching. It is healing, it is therapeutic. It is nurturing and maturing. It is preaching that is concerned about people, that meets deep human needs. It is made possible by infusing great biblical themes that nurture the congregation with pastoral concern.

I think pastoral preaching is absolutely necessary since it meets three basic needs of people.

First, people need support. Many who come to worship are like people treading water. They are fighting hard to keep their heads above water, and the slightest thing can shove them under. They need a hand put beneath their armpits to lift them up. Pastoral preaching gives such a hand. It keeps them from going under, from drowning.

A pastor should be aware that there is a kind of preaching that shoves people under, and often there are those who want this kind of preaching. Such preaching is a false way of meeting guilt in the near drowning.

Through pastoral preaching a pastor is not only offering support, he is helping to develop a church that offers support—a church that puts strong hands beneath the armpits of those who are about to sink, a church that will lay steadying hands on shaky lives, a church that will walk with the lonely and forsaken.

Henri Nouwen in his book, *The Wounded Healer,* speaks of how life is bereft of meaning without a brother or sister. A person can keep his sanity and meaning for life if he knows that at least one person is waiting for him. No tomorrow is too forbidding to be entered if there is somebody to walk with you. But when nobody is waiting the odds are too great. You go down in the struggle. There is no reason to live if there is nobody to live with and for. Thousands of people, he says, commit suicide because they envision a future with nobody there.

The supporting church puts somebody in a person's future. I will not let him envision a future with nobody there.

Second, people need a sense of worth, importance, and dignity.

I have done a lot of counseling over a rather long ministry and about ten years ago concluded that I had never worked with an emotionally distraught person who didn't have a poor self-image either at the center of his problem or as a responsible factor. Somehow the conclusion didn't seem valid, but when I checked it out with a professional psychologist, he said that that had been his experience, too.

So many people feel hollow, empty, washed out, guilty, useless, and worthless. I believe that everybody struggles with this problem at times in one's life. Possibly the poor self-image is everyone's story.

We have said that the basic human problem is the sin of pride. But the opposite may be just as true. How often we lick the dust when we should stand to our feet and be somebody. We need to know ourselves as persons of worth. Jesus said we were to love ourselves. Unless we can do that we can't give a healthy love to others. If we can't see beauty in ourselves we can't see it in others.

Who is better able to affirm the worth of people than the pastor who stands in the pulpit? A congregation, facing their pastor, should have a feeling that, if articulated, would say: "There is a person who loves us, affirms our worth, and believes we are important."

In pastoral preaching, the pastor helps to grow a church that affirms the worth and dignity of people. When a church is authentic, everybody in its life is somebody.

Paul in the twelfth chapter of 1 Corinthians speaks of the church as the body of Christ. Believers compose the body of Christ the way limbs and organs made up the physical body. He talks about how each member has an indispensable role: "The eye cannot say to the hand, 'I have no need of you,' nor again the head to the feet, 'I have no need of you.'" Then he says a most wonderful thing: "On the contrary, the parts of the body which seem to be weaker are indispensable" (vv. 21-22). Paul does not say that these seemingly insignificant organs are important, that they would be missed if they were lost. He says they are indispensable! It is that way when the church is what Christ wants it to be. The smallest, least powerful, person in the church is indispensable. If he moves away, something of the church leaves us. If he dies, something of the church dies. The pastor through his preaching seeks to create this kind of church that affirms the indispensable worth and value of everyone. Everybody is somebody.

Third, people need to grow up and become mature in Christ.

One of the tragedies of the Christian life is that so many people experience stunted and arrested growth. They don't grow up. Although they may become cultured, intellectual, and professional giants, they remain spiritual midgets.

One of the things that Paul lamented about the church at Corinth was that they had not grown, but were still babies in Christ. He was still giving them milk. They couldn't take the solid food.

While I was a student in New York City in 1941 I often passed Jack Dempsey's restaurant on Broadway. I always looked to see Dempsey and often did. I could understand why he had been the world's heavyweight boxing champion. He was a perfect specimen of physical manhood. One day I saw a great crowd pressing against the window of the restaurant looking in. Being curious to know what had attracted them, I elbowed my way through the crowd and looked in where I saw the attraction—two midgets talking with Dempsey. The contrast was startling. Dempsey was so big and strong, and they were so small. How often in their spiritual lives people are like those midgets.

Jesus told Peter to feed his lambs. He knew that if he did the lambs would grow.

Paul, in the fourth chapter of Ephesians, points to the goal to which every pastor should be leading his people: "Until we all attain to the unity of the faith and of the knowledge of the Son of God, to mature manhood, to the measure of the stature of the fulness of Christ; so that we may no longer be children, tossed to and fro and carried about with every wind of doctrine, by the cunning of men, by their craftiness in deceitful wiles. Rather, speaking the truth in love, we are to grow up in every way into him who is the head, into Christ" (Eph. 4:13-15).

The end is mature, full-grown men and women. What is this maturity? Paul doesn't spell it out, maybe he comes near to it when he said we are to speak the truth in love. That certainly is a worthy end. Do you know how dangerous truth is unless spoken in love? You can demolish people with it. It can be a terrible vice. But that is true of every other virtue, not in the keeping of love. No virtue is safe except in the hands of love.

The ultimate end of every pastor is to lead his people to spiritual maturity, to arrive at the place where they will speak the truth in love, and live the truth in love. Pastoral preaching will help him or her achieve that end.

WHAT MAKES IT POSSIBLE?

At least five things make pastoral preaching possible.

First, love Christ and accept him as your model.

Jesus in his conversation with Peter in the early morning along the seashore didn't ask him if he would love those entrusted to his care. He asked Peter if he would love him best of all. This didn't mean that Peter would not love his flock. Indeed, because he loved Jesus first he would love his people more and in ways he never could have if he had not given priority to Jesus.

We can never see the beauty and possibilities of a human face until the light that shone in the eyes of Jesus falls upon it. Here is a scarred, hideous face that has always been repulsive to me. Then one day the light that was in Christ falls on that face and for the first time I see how beautiful it can be.

Jesus Christ is to be our model. We are to see people as he did, love them the way he did, and respond to them the way he did.

It is not enough to say that the Christian pastor loves people. That can be said about anybody. There should be an extra dimension in his love. He should love people the way Jesus did.

Christ is looking for channels through which to pour his love for the healing of the brokenness of life. What better channel should there be than a Christian pastor?

Again, preach biblical themes, infused with pastoral concern, that are nurturing. Preach on the initiative and priority of God's love. He loved us first, therefore we can love him. Preach on the worth, value, and dignity of human life. We find our real worth in that we are made in the image of God and that we are infinitely loved by God.

Preach on faith, hope, love, and service. Preach on self-denial, discipline, and sacrifice. This style of life certainly speaks of maturity. Preach on the devotional life, on prayer and worship.

Preach on belonging to the church as the people of God. We cannot mature in isolation. We need those who will call us by name, reach out and touch us, strike a cadence and walk with us. We need the kind of social relations that are found within the community of Christ.

Preach on social responsibility and commitment. Only as we are drawn from out of ourselves, from beyond ourselves, only as we give ourselves to something great, can we grow up.

Preach on the great doctrines of the church. This may sound strange, but to know these doctrines gives stability which is one of the marks of maturity. Indeed, Paul pointed to instability in matters of doctrine as one of the marks of immaturity. "So that we may no longer be children," he wrote, "tossed to and fro and carried about with every wind of doctrine" (Eph. 4:14).

Further, as earlier suggested, be human. Unless we admit our humanity, we cannot understand the struggle, pain, hope, and doubt of our people and we can't speak to their needs.

Yet, there is a strong temptation for the pastor to deny his humanity. Too often his people will not see him as being thoroughly human, and all too often he accepts that image for himself. He is neither human nor divine. He is suspended somewhere between heaven and earth. In a sense, this position is a safe place. He does not run the risk of vulnerability. But if it is a safe place, it is a lonely place. This is one of the reasons so many pastors are lonely. The ministry is sometimes spoken of as the lonely profession. But worst of all, this position is a false place. It is a living lie. We are human and this is a denial of it. All too often a pastor breaks beneath the tension existing between who he appears to be and who he really is.

Next to the grace of God, humanity is our greatest asset in the pulpit. The brokenness of our humanity can be like crevices through which the grace of Christ is poured like summer showers on parched ground.

Once more, you have to know your people. Preaching is bifocal. It involves the gospel that is preached and the people to whom the gospel is preached. The minister who does pastoral preaching must know his gospel and his people. Which is more important? That is like asking which focus in an ellipse is more important. There is a sense in which one is as important as the other. Take one focus away—it doesn't matter which—and the ellipse will collapse. You can't have an ellipse without both foci. Just so, we can't do effective pastoral preaching unless the minister knows both his gospel and his people and how to bring them together.

How will a pastor know his people? In essentially two ways. First, he will have to come down from his suspended position and touch the common earth. He will have to declare his humanity. He will have to unmask himself. Unless he is willing to do this his people will not unmask themselves. He has to be knowable if he is to know his people.

The pastor will also have to be with his people, especially during crises. If he is willing to be with them in their failure, pain, sickness, and death, when the defenses are down, he can know them. Doors will be open that may never be open again. He should enter them. He will be privileged to walk around on the interior of their lives which is sacred ground. He should never tell what he sees and hears there.

Finally, you must love your people.

No matter how eloquent, knowledgeable, and gifted a minister is, he cannot do effective pastoral preaching unless he loves his people. On the other hand, he may be missing in eloquence and other gifts, yet do effective pastoral preaching if his people feel warmth, love, acceptance, and concern in him. And the pastor cannot fake this. It has to be real and genuine. Pious words and gestures do not necessarily indicate a loving heart. If a pastor has a loving heart, he doesn't have to be gushing and sentimental. The people will know it.

Leslie Weatherhead once wrote: "Be relevant, be simple, and then I would say be loving. I think the most beautiful thing ever said about a preacher was this. Somebody said: 'Why is it that he has such power over people, and why do they come so far to hear him?' And the answer was: 'He puts his arms around the whole congregation and no one feels left out.'. . . The great preachers have been great lovers. The great preachers have been people who made simple, homely folk, such as you and me, feel they were loved."[2]

Robert J. McCracken wrote about Dick Sheppard, a famous English preacher during the first quarter of this century. Plagued with illness, he often prayed the asthmatic's prayer, "Give us this day our daily breath." In addition he carried a personal cross heavier than his asthma: His wife was unfaithful to him. Weakened physically and emotionally, he gave himself unsparingly to his people. Frequently he would sit up all night with a sick parishioner. When he was dean of Canterbury he would be up by six-thirty in the morning to meet the cathedral workers as they began their day's work. He loved people and their concerns became his own. He was never a stranger to pain and suffering. When he died, an East London dock worker said, "Good Gawd, Mother, what shall we do without 'im?" And when people heard of his death they found themselves saying not how fond they were of him, but how fond he was of them. McCracken believed that this fellow feeling, this identification with human need, was the great strength of his preaching and the secret of his hold on people.[3]

I remember Jim Barbour who was struck down by death in the midst of his best years. Jim loved his people, and they came first. I used to see him in the hospital at all hours of the day and night, caring for sick members of his church. It didn't matter what he was doing—reading an exciting book, preparing next

Sunday's sermon, or in a devotional period—he left immediately to get to the person who needed him. His preaching was basically pastoral, and he could do it with real effectiveness. He had met the conditions.

This pastoral love expresses itself in terms of sympathy and love.

John A. Broadus, the great preacher and writer about preaching, once said: "If I were asked what is the first thing in effective preaching, I should say sympathy; and what is the second thing, I would say sympathy, and what is the third thing. I would say sympathy."[4]

PASTORAL PREACHING AND OTHER KINDS

There are many ways of classifying preaching, but I like to think of three basic kinds—evangelistic, prophetic, and pastoral. I know of course, that this classification is not exhaustive. At one end of the preaching spectrum is evangelistic preaching, at the other end is prophetic, and at the center is pastoral preaching.

I have a simple theory about preaching: The best way to do effective evangelistic and prophetic preaching is to first do effective pastoral preaching.

In evangelistic preaching we announce the good news that God loves us in spite of our sin, brokenness, and alienation. God's love does not in any sense depend on our beauty, goodness, and worth. He loves us because he is God. He can't help loving us. God sought us in Christ and found us in our loneliest and most desperate situation. We in our desperation struck the hand that would heal us and spurned the love that would save us. We could not stand him. His goodness uncovered the evil in us, his love judged our lovelessness and hatred, and the light that was in him exposed the shadows and darkness of our minds. Christ got caught in the cross fire of our hurt, fear, hatred, and evil. He gave his life, and in so doing accomplished a most wonderful thing: In his death he bore our sin and carried our shame far away. Because he did, salvation is a gift of grace. God bids us come just as we are, not waiting until we are older, wiser, or better, and accept his salvation. We come with empty hands and God puts in them his gift of grace.

Prophetic preaching, as we have already said, addresses the gospel to our corporate life. There we do without shame and blushing what would be very abhorrent to us in our more personal life. We are most sinful in the things we do together. God strongly judges us in the prophetic word. But the prophetic word is also a word of hope, forgiveness, renewal, and new beginnings are offered.

Why is it that pastoral preaching puts us in a position to do more effective evangelistic preaching on one hand and more effective prophetic preaching on the other?

To repeat, pastoral preaching is accepting, supportive, and nurturing. Therefore, in pastoral preaching the pastor expresses love, acceptance, and compassion. He who does that can best tell the sinner that God loves, accepts, and forgives him in Christ. A preacher can bear witness most effectively to the love of Christ if people have first felt that love in him. Let him who would be an evangelist first do well his task of pastoral preaching.

As already indicated, prophetic preaching can be highly disruptive. But effective pastoral preaching makes possible prophetic preaching without tragic disruptions for two reasons: Pastoral preaching is confessional and it is able to establish those deep relationships that can stand the shock and absorb the stress of the prophetic voice.

Pastoral preaching demands that a preacher declare his own humanity. Having done that, he can never pose in the pulpit as a sinless person hurling judgments at his people. He is one sinner preaching to other sinners. He confesses his own involvement in the sinful entanglements of life. There is nothing more disarming than a preacher who has the courage to do confessional preaching.

Pastoral preaching alone can create the depths of relationships so necessary for prophetic preaching that is healing and not tragically disruptive.

We greatly need prophetic preaching in our time, but often the pulpit is silent on crucial issues. It seems that almost everything speaks to them except the pulpit. That is tragic. The people have a right to expect a hero in the pulpit, and it is too bad when they see a timid and cowardly man who is afraid of his own shadow. But let him who would be a prophet first be a pastor, and let him who would do prophetic preaching first do pastoral preaching.

Those of us who are pastors could enjoy no higher calling. Having been called to be pastors, we need to do whatever we can do pastorally. That means, among other things, that we are to do pastoral preaching. Let us do it well.

15
Taking Thought for Tomorrow's Preaching

One of the most important and challenging, yet difficult, tasks of the preacher is the preparation of sermons. It is important because we have been given a crucially vital word to speak. The word entrusted to us is so important that life really doesn't make sense until we hear and obey it. It is challenging because we are speaking that word to the same congregation once, twice, or maybe even more times each week. How do we keep that word authoritative, fresh, and in touch with the lives of our people? How do we avoid repetition, imbalance, irrelevance, and boredom in the pulpit? We often feel that we are challenged by an impossible task. Who else except a preacher would undertake that kind of thing?

Any preacher who uses a slipshod, freewheeling, week by week method of preparation is in trouble. He lays waste energy that is not productive because he does not properly channel it. He proves unfair to himself, the word he is called to proclaim, and the people to whom he preaches.

The best possible answer to the problem, it seems to me, is to lay out a planned, long-range pulpit ministry. By so doing we take thought for tomorrow's preaching.

WEEK-BY-WEEK PREPARATION

Before we go further let us give some additional thought to week by week preparation without a long-range plan.

Many a pastor completes his Sunday's sermon with a sigh of relief. It is over with and he is glad, but Monday is soon there and staring him in the face is the question: What shall I preach next Sunday? That question may be a shadow of anxiety that lies heavy over the beginning of the week. It is a hard enough task if he has only one sermon to prepare. It may be an intolerable burden if he has two.

The week quickly speeds by. Wednesday morning is soon here when he must prepare the material for his church bulletin. He has had no moment of inspiration and he is unable to announce his sermon title for next Sunday. So he simply puts down: Sermon by the Pastor. Thursday and Friday pass, and Saturday morning is here. Still no moment of inspiration. No great truth has claimed his mind, but he must produce within twenty-four hours. A mild panic may be working on him now. He frantically reads some Scripture, but still no ideas. Saturday night comes. By now he is desperate. There are only two alternatives left to him: Go to the sermon barrels or preach another person's sermon.

The sermon barrel can be a dangerous place. It can be a refuge to which we flee when under the pressure of emptiness. It is indeed sad for a preacher to use an old sermon with hackneyed and platitudinous language, preaching it to a congregation that has moved on from where the first congregation was. His people are worthy of better pulpit fare and should have it.

The second alternative may be even worse. It is especially bad when a preacher uses another person's sermon without giving him credit for it. We call it plagiarism which is really a euphemism for stealing. When we use another person's ideas without giving him credit, we steal from him. One is afraid that this is practiced much more widely in our pulpits than is believed.

I remember a very fine institute I was attending about ten years ago. One evening a widely-known minister from a prominent church in the Northeast was preaching. As he spoke, I had the feeling that there was something very familiar about what he was saying, but it was a passing thought. I had a friend at the institute who was publishing rather widely, and I found him very agitated at the end of the service. He said, "The speaker this evening preached one of my sermons, which was recently published, word for word. He even told my personal illustrations as if they were his own." (I understood then why the material had sounded so familiar—I had read the sermon.) My friend confronted the minister with his plagiarism in the presence of the director of the institute, and he did not deny it. The word got out, and it cast a pall of sadness over the conference. It was not just that this man had violated the ethics of the pulpit; it awakened the suspicion that this kind of thing happens all too frequently.

Every preacher should have written in bold letters the Seventh Commandment across his mentality: "You shall not steal" (Ex. 20:15). The question asked by Paul to self-righteous Jews may well be asked of us: "You then who teach others, will you not teach yourself? While you preach against stealing, do you steal?" (Rom. 2:21).

This is not to suggest that we are not to use other people's ideas. How can we escape that? No person is sufficiently gifted and creative enough to make sure that all of his ideas are original. The truth is we borrow, we have to borrow. Many ideas have been woven into our mental fabric the sources of which we do not know nor remember. We cannot give credit for these. But when we do know the sources, as often we do, we are ethically bound to acknowledge them.

J. Randall Nichols tells of a seminary course which was developed in order to help students use other preachers' sermons honestly and creatively as appropriate tools for ministry. "The basic idea is simplicity itself," he writes. "A preacher announces that on a given Sunday he or she will be delivering the sermon of a certain other preacher (having secured necessary permission, of course, in conformity with copyright laws). An explanatory note about the original author and the circumstances of the sermon (if known) is printed in the Sunday bulletin. . . . Instead of plagiarism, we have a unique teaching opportunity. The only thing standing between plagiarism and using other sermons responsibly and creatively is acknowledgement."[1]

If we should take Nichols seriously we might well improve our preaching and at the same time keep honest in the pulpit. We could make it possible for our people to hear some of the world's greatest sermons.

LONG-RANGE PLANNING

I recently attended a two-week conference on theology and preaching at a nationally-recognized seminary. One day at lunch we met a young man whom we had not seen in our classes and workshops. He told us that he was using the library in preparing a year's pulpit ministry. "It enables me to survive," he said. No one could mistake the value he put on long-range planning.

I am suggesting that long-range planning is at least a partial answer to ministers who find themselves in exhausting, anxiety-producing predicaments in their sermon preparation.

How do you go about long-range planning? How do you take thought for tomorrow's preaching? Let me make three suggestions.

First, preach series of sermons.

Series of sermons have almost unlimited possibilities. They afford a wide range of interesting materials, which can throw into focus the great biblical, theological, devotional, ethical, and social themes of our faith.

We are living through a time of theological illiteracy. So many people are Christians but do not know why they are. It is a time when we need doctrinal preaching. A series of sermons on

Christian doctrine would be very helpful. Such a series could be given under the general theme, "On Being Doctrinally Literate." This series would allow us to throw into focus the great doctrines of the Christian church. These doctrines should be presented in such a way as to show that our faith did not come from intellectual speculation, but from disclosures, events, meetings, experience, and life. Having come from life, they must pass back into life. Our doctrines are to be lived, else doctrinal preaching will be deadening to the person in the pulpit and boring to those in the pew.

A series of sermons can be developed from books of the Bible. What about a series from the Psalms under the theme, "Hymns from the World's Greatest Hymnal"? No literature of the Bible runs a wider spectrum of human experience and touches more deeply the interior of the human heart. Nothing in the world's literature knows better the hope and hopelessness, the joy and anguish of human life. The Psalms will not accept simplistic answers to the agonizing questions about life and God. They put us in touch with our feelings and demand that we be honest with them.

The Bible asks the right questions about the significance of life and asks them in a searching and probing way. Take for example the question the people were asking on Palm Sunday: "Who is this?" (Matt. 21:10); or the question the lawyer asked Jesus: "Who is my neighbor?" (Luke 10:29). A series of exciting sermons could be developed on the theme, "Questions the Bible Asks."

The answers the Bible gives are just as significant as the questions it asks. Take for example Peter's answer to Jesus' question concerning who he was: "You are the Christ, the Son of the living God" (Matt. 16:16); or Paul and Silas's answer to the Philippian jailer: "Believe in the Lord Jesus, and you will be saved, you and your household" (Acts 16:31). The answers of the Bible are like keys that unlock the meaning of life, like shafts of light that fall into the mystery of life, and like signs along the roads of life pointing us to our destination. Why not do a series on "Answers the Bible Gives"?

The Bible is a great devotional book. Even where there are not prayers, much of the material is written devotionally. Many of the prayers are deeply moving, touching the deepest devotional springs of the heart. Moses' prayer, for example, for his liberated people so soon returned to idolatry, must be the greatest intercessory prayer ever offered: "Alas, this people have sinned a great sin; they have made themselves gods of gold. But now, if thou wilt forgive their sin—and if not, blot me, I pray thee, out of thy book which thou has written" (Ex. 32:31-32). A series on the "Prayers of the Bible" could be very enriching.

The doxologies of the Bible are among its most beautiful and moving devotional literature. In the seventh chapter of Revelation we get a picture of the church in its perfection. They came from everywhere, "a great multitude which no man could number" (v. 9). They represent all nations and peoples. All barriers have been broken down. They are dressed in white robes having been cleansed by the blood of Christ. They have been busy about the main task of the church, that of reconciliation, and hold in their hands palm branches which are symbols of peace. And with a loud voice they are singing a doxology: "Salvation belongs to our God who sits upon the throne, and to the Lamb!" (v. 10). And those about the throne are singing a doxology: "Amen! Blessing and glory and wisdom and thanksgiving and honor and power and might be to our God forever and ever! Amen." (v. 12). Can you imagine how exciting a series of sermons could be on "The Doxologies of the Bible"?

The benedictions of the Bible have as fine a quality as the doxologies. Hear this one: "Now may the God of peace who brought again from the dead our Lord Jesus, the great shepherd of the sheep by the blood of the eternal covenant, equip you with everything good that you may do his will, working in you that which is pleasing in his sight, through Jesus Christ; to whom be glory for ever and ever. Amen" (Heb. 13:20-21). I think the most appropriate way to begin a service of worship is to sing a doxology, and the most appropriate way to end a service is to give a benediction. It is meaningful to send forth a congregation from a sanctuary back into the busy world with the peace and blessing of Almighty God upon them. Do you see the possibilities of a series of sermons on the "Benedictions of the Bible"?

Christian truth, while it can be abstract, usually comes to us in very concrete forms. Because of this it is often mediated through persons. Remember how the author of Hebrews begins his great book: "In many and various ways God spoke of old to our fathers by the prophets; but in these last days, he has spoken to us by a Son" (1:1-2). God comes to us and speaks to us in person, especially one person, Jesus Christ. Why not do a series on the great characters of the Bible under the theme, "Lengthened Shadows Across Our Landscape"? Names rush in upon your mind: Abraham, Joseph, Moses, Isaiah, Jeremiah, Amos, Micah, Hosea, Peter, John, Paul, Jesus, and many more.

One is impressed with the meetings and encounters of the Bible. They are often decisive. A series of sermons on "Meetings That Made a Difference" could be very revealing. These encounters would involve the meeting of people with people and the meeting of people with God. Think of Moses meeting God in a burning bush, Amos meeting God while he followed his flock, or Saul of Tarsus meeting the living Christ along the Damascus road. Some encounters may be purely human, yet point beyond themselves. Take for example Jacob's meeting his brother Esau after an absence of twenty years. Jacob had fled for his life, fearing the anger and rage of Esau, who could be like a wild man, and he was afraid to meet Esau again. But Jacob was greatly surprised. He found Esau gracious and loving, and Jacob said to his brother: "For truly to see your face is like seeing the face of God, with such favor you received me" (Gen. 33:10). What a story!

We speak of Christianity as being a historical religion. The sphere of God's revelation, as earlier said, is not the heavens but the dusty ways of our human pilgrimage. God acts in history. Events, therefore, are very important in our religion. A series of sermons on "Events That Shape History" could be very engaging. Such events as the call of Abraham, the Exodus, the giving of the law and the covenant, the second exodus from Babylonian captivity, the birth of Jesus, the death of Jesus, the resurrection of Jesus, the gift of the Spirit and Pentecost, and others could be used.

The Bible, as earlier discussed, often uses metaphor and symbol. These can speak of reality—and it is the most important kind of reality—that eludes our prosaic and scientific languages. Light is one of the favorite metaphors of the Bible and helps form one of its basic motifs. Why not develop a series of sermons on "The Light That Does Not Go Out." The Bible begins with light which was the first thing God created and ends with a city perfectly lighted, not having a shadow or trace of darkness in it. You recall how the children of Israel were led by a pillar of fire by night. The Word of God is spoken of as a lamp to our feet and a light to our path (Ps. 119:105). Remember the significance of light in the beautiful stories about the birth of Jesus and how the stories of the resurrection are set in the light of early morning. Jesus said he was the light of the world and God is defined as being light in whom there is no darkness at all. It is the great privilege and mission of the church to "declare the wonderful deeds of him who called you out of darkness into his marvelous light" (1 Peter 2:9).

We must not neglect the ethical and social dimensions of our gospel. The spiritual and ethical, the personal and the social are inseparable, bound up together like the back and palm of my hand. If I try to separate the back from the palm I succeed only in getting a mutilated hand. When we seek to separate the personal from the social in our faith we get a mutilated gospel. A series of sermons "The Moral Imperatives of the Bible" would be timely. Our Scripture abounds in such great texts as these: "Cease to do evil,/learn to do good" (Isa. 1:16b-17a); "Let justice roll down like waters,/and righteousness like an ever-flowing stream" (Amos 5:24); "He has showed you, O man, what is good;/and what does the Lord require of you/but to do justice, and to love kindness,/and to walk humbly with your God?" (Micah 6:8); "You tithe mint and dill and cummin, and have neglected the weightier matters of the law, justice and mercy and faith" (Matt. 23:23); "A new commandment I give to you, that you love one another; even as I have loved you, that you also love one another" (John 13:34); "This commandment we have from him, that he who loves God should love his brother also" (1 John 4:21).

Second, the use of a lectionary.

A lectionary is a list of Scripture selections for each Sunday set within the church (Christian) year. There are three selections for each Sunday—from the Old Testament, Epistles, and Gospels, with the exception of Eastertide, when Old Testament readings are omitted. Occasionally readings from Acts and Revelation are substituted for Epistles. The Scripture selections reach their climax in the reading from one of the Gospels. Just as Christ is climactic to God's revelation, the Gospels are climactic to the whole of Scripture.

The Christian year is indeed an old, interesting, and significant calendar. It has seven seasons: Advent, Christmastide, Epiphany, Lent, Holy Week, Eastertide, and Pentecost with the Sundays lying between Pentecost and Advent. The Christian year starts with Advent, which begins the Sunday nearest November 30 (fourth Sunday before Christmas), and continues to the Sunday before Christmas.

Advent is a season of looking, expectancy, and hope. We are looking for somebody, and if he comes all things will be different. It is one of the most joyous seasons when the Church remembers most joyfully the coming of Christ, expects new comings of grace into our lives, and looks forward to the second coming of Christ.

Christmastide is the festival of Christ's birth when we celebrate the Incarnation. It is a twelve-day period from December 25 to January 5, and may include either one or two Sundays after Christmas.

Epiphany begins January 6 which celebrates the revealing of Christ to the Gentiles in the person of the Magi. The season continues to Ash Wednesday, which begins Lent, and can include from four to nine Sundays.

Lent is a period of forty weekdays and six Sundays, beginning with Ash Wednesday and culminating in Holy Week. The church in joy and sorrow, proclaims, remembers, and responds to the atoning death of Jesus Christ.

Holy Week is the week prior to Easter, beginning with Palm Sunday, when the church gratefully commemorates the passion and death of Jesus Christ.

Eastertide is a fifty-day period of seven Sundays, beginning with Easter, the festival of Christ's resurrection. Ascension Day, forty days after Easter, is celebrated in the affirmation that Jesus Christ is Lord of all times and places.

Pentecost, when we celebrate the gift of the Spirit to the Church, is an extended season, beginning with the seventh Sunday after Easter to the beginning of Advent. During this season, which is roughly one half of the church year, we reflect on how God's people are to live under the guidance of the Spirit.

It is interesting to note that the first half of the church year is festive in nature when we celebrate great events of the Christian faith. Preaching will be related to these events. The second half is nonfestive. The thinking is less event-centered and more thematic. This season allows for a wide range of preaching on doctrinal, ethical, and social concerns.

One popular current lectionary is an adaptation of the Roman Catholic Church lectionary and is used by the Lutheran, Episcopal, Presbyterian, United Church of Christ, as well as other churches. It has been prepared for a three-year cycle in series A, B, and C.

There are certain obvious advantages in using a lectionary. It allows for long-range planning. It keeps before us the great events and themes of the Christian faith. It makes for balanced biblical preaching. It may be the cure for a dangerous subjectivism. With a lectionary before us there is a sense in which the Scriptures choose us. It helps remind us that God has other children with long histories who are still with us and who join us in the enterprise of the Kingdom.

But there are also certain disadvantages in using a lectionary. It is easy to let the lectionary master us rather than our mastering it. If slavishly followed, it does not sufficiently allow for the novel, the spontaneous, and the current that may beg for attention. Important passages of Scripture have to be omitted of necessity, and the lessons on a given Sunday may not grip and inspire us. Sometimes there is a hermeneutic that sees the Old Testament fulfilled in the new in a way that does violence to the Old Testament.

Third, planning a year's pulpit ministry.

Almost forty years ago Andrew W. Blackwood, great teacher of homiletics at Princeton Theological Seminary, wrote a book, *Planning a Year's Pulpit Work*. The book has been far-reaching in its influence and has inspired many pastors to plan their pulpit ministries a year in advance.

At first you may be overwhelmed by the task. It may seem impossible. If so, I have an encouraging word for you. You can do it with considerable ease.

How do you go about it? I would suggest that you take four

calendars—the church year, the civil calendar, the denominational calendar, and the local church calendar—and lay them side by side. Then begin lifting from these calendars important days. The church year can be especially helpful for the festival seasons of Advent, Christmas, Epiphany, Lent, Holy Week, Easter, Ascension Day, and Pentecost Sunday. The great redemptive deeds of our faith are thrown into clear focus in this part of the church year.

Adopt from the civil calendar such emphases as New Year's Day, Brotherhood Week, Memorial Day, Mother's Day, Father's Day, Independence Day, Labor Day, and Thanksgiving Day.

Such days and emphases on the following should be lifted from the denominational calendar: prayer for foreign missions, prayer for home missions, prayer for state missions, Christian Education Sunday, Christian Home Week, Race Relations Sunday, World Hunger Day, and World Communion Sunday.

Then your local church calendar will suggest certain days and emphases: Promotion Sunday, stewardship, evangelism, Youth Sunday, Senior Citizen Sunday, Denominational Sunday, Bible Study Week, and others. What about the Sundays when you observe communion? These should be carefully guarded.

You will discover that your pulpit ministry will be overcrowded. There will be more special days and special themes than you can handle. Then comes the setting of your priorities, sifting, and cutting down. After having chosen your themes and emphases for the Sundays of the year, you will select appropriate Scripture lessons and texts. Initial insights, impressions, and directions will also be listed with each theme. Then these will be filed chronologically. You will discover that during the year relevant ideas from your reading, reflection, observation, and experience will often come with compelling power. These ideas should be entered appropriately in your file before they lose their freshness or are forgotten. You can then begin concentrating on sermon preparation without the loss of time and energy that results from a more slipshod method. What a relief it is to know where you are going. And often, as you sit down to prepare next Sunday's sermon, you will be surprised to see the amount of material already gathered.

There is a word of caution. Master the plan without letting it master you; be flexible in the use of it; be open to new situations you could not possibly have anticipated when you were arranging the schedule; and always be sensitive to the novel and spontaneous.

It should be said in closing that unless you have a strong sense of calling and a high concept of preaching, nothing can save you, not even a year's pulpit plan. The sermon will still be a chore set in the midst of a busy week. But if you can feel with Jeremiah that God has put the words on your lips, if you believe that the voice of the preacher was heard when the church was being born, has been heard ever since with varying degrees of clarity and force, and must continue to be heard if the church is to have life and vitality, then a planned pulpit program will help you channel your energy in fulfilling the most important task ever given a person.

NOTES

Chapter 1
   1. Dwight E. Stevenson and Charles F. Kiehl, *Reaching People from the Pulpit* (Grand Rapids: Baker Book House, 1958), p. 173.
   2. Clyde E. Fant, Jr., and William M. Pinson, Jr., *Twenty Centuries of Great Preaching* Vol. 1 (Waco, Texas: Word Books, 1979), p. 99.

Chapter 2
   1. J. H. Jowett, *The Preacher: His Life and Work* (Grand Rapids: Baker Book House, reprinted from the original edition, 1912), p. 125.

Chapter 3
   1. Stevenson and Kiehl, *Reaching People from the Pulpit*, p. 66.
   2. Frederick Buechner, *Telling the Truth: The Gospel as Tragedy, Comedy, and Fairy Tale* (New York: Harper and Row, 1977), pp. 7, 50.

Chapter 4
   1. John A. Broadus, *On the Preparation and Delivery of Sermons,* (New York: Harper and Row, 1979), p. 202.
   2. D. W. Cleverly Ford, *Preaching Today* (Epworth Press and SPCK, 1969), p. 56.
   3. Frederick Buechner, *Telling the Truth*, p. 19.
   4. Ibid., p. 25.
   5. Fant and Pinson, Ibid., pp. 211, 215.
   6. Ibid., Vol. IX, p. 183.
   7. Ibid., Vol. I, pp. 211, 215.

8. Charles R. Brown, *The Art of Preaching* (New York: The Macmillan Company, 1849), p. 181.

9. H. Grady Davis, *Design for Preaching* (Philadelphia: Fortress Press, 1958), pp. 271-272.

10. Brown, Ibid., p. 182.

11. Jowett, Ibid., p. 140.

Chapter 5

1. Fant and Pinson, Ibid., Vol. XII, p. 154.

Chapter 6

1. Richard A. Jensen, *Telling the Story* (Minneapolis: Augsburg Publishing House, 1979), p. 116.

2. *The Christian Century,* May 14, 1980, p. 548.

3. Henry H. Mitchell, *The Recovery of Preaching* (New York: Harper and Row, 1977), p. 155.

4. Edmund A. Steimle, Morris J. Niedenthal, and Charles L. Rice, *Preaching the Story* (Philadelphia: Fortress Press, 1980), p. 171.

5. Mitchell, Ibid., p. 158.

Chapter 7

1. Ford, Ibid., p. 30.

2. Ibid., pp. 30-31.

3. Donald G. Miller, *The Presbyterian Outlook,* January 10, 1977.

4. Chevis F. Horne, *Crisis in the Pulpit* (Grand Rapids: Baker Book House, 1975), pp. 68-70.

Chapter 8

1. William E. Sangster, *The Craft of Sermon Construction* (Grand Rapids: Baker Book House, 1979), p. 13.

2. *The Interpreter's Bible,* Vol. VII (Nashville and New York: Abingdon-Cokesbury Press, 1956), p. 335.

3. David H. C. Read, *Sent from God* (Nashville and New York: Abingdon Press, 1974), pp. 68-69.

4. Jowett, Ibid., p. 143.

5. Sangster, Ibid., p. 189.

6. Jowett, Ibid., p. 151.

7. Robert J. McCracken, *The Making of the Sermon* (New York: Harper and Brothers, 1956), p. 16.

Chapter 9
1. Gardner C. Taylor, *How Shall They Preach?* (Elgin, Ill.: Progressive Baptist Publishing House, 1977), p. 45.
2. Fant and Pinson, Ibid., Vol. I, p. vii.
3. Ibid., Vol. IX, p. 155.
4. *Time* magazine, December 3, 1979.
5. Jowett, Ibid., p. 136-137.
6. Fant and Pinson, Ibid., Vol. X, pp. 264-265.
7. Robert McAfee Brown, *The Bible Speaks to You* (Philadelphia: Westminster Press, 1955), p. 17.
8. Chevis F. Horne, Ibid., pp. 48-49.

Chapter 10
1. Read, Ibid., pp. 31, 107.
2. Clyde E. Fant, *Preaching for Today* (New York: Harper and Row, 1975), pp. xiv., 29.

Chapter 11
1. Fant and Pinson, Ibid., Vol. IX, p. 17.
2. Read, Ibid., p. 199.
3. John McKay, *God's Order* (London: Nisbet and Company, LTD, 1953), p. 42.

Chapter 14
1. Fant and Pinson, Ibid., Vol. X, p. 344.
2. Fant and Pinson, Ibid., Vol. XI, p. 113.
3. Horne, Ibid., p. 45.
4. Edgar Dewitt Jones, *The Royalty of the Pulpit* (New York: Harper and Brothers, 1951), p. 55.

Chapter 15
1. J. Randall Nichols, *Building the Word* (San Francisco: Harper and Row, 1980), p. 147.

251
H 815D

70672